P9-EJI-351

SNIPER

SNIPER

Peter Brookesmith

THOMAS
DUNNE
BOOKS

ST. MARTIN'S PRESS 🙢 NEW YORK

THOMAS DUNNE BOOKS
An imprint of St. Martin's Press.

ISBN: 0-312-26098-9

First U.S. Edition 2000

Editorial and design by
Amber Books Ltd
Bradley's Close
74–77 White Lion Street
London N1 9PF

Project editor: Brian Burns
Design: Brian Rust

Printed in Italy

10 9 8 7 6 5 4 3 2 1

Contents

CHAPTER 1

THE SNIPER IN HISTORY

The development of the sniper's art

'There is no hunting like the hunting of man, and those who have hunted armed men long enough and liked it, never care for anything else thereafter.'
—*Ernest Hemingway*

The entire concept of sniping is derived from hunting. English dictionaries cannot resist associating the term 'sniper' with the snipe, a small wading bird of the genus *Gallinago* that is to be found on foreshores, marshes and other damp ground in many countries. There seems to be some justification for making the connection, for the snipe is a speedy bird, easily alarmed, flying in a rocking, nearly spiral path that makes it exceptionally difficult to shoot. During the eighteenth century, hunting the bird with guns became a favourite if demanding pastime of British army officers in India, and the term 'sniper' gradually came into general use, meaning a cunning stalker and an expert shot. The first written use of the word in this sense appears as early as 1773, in a soldier's letter from India. The Oxford English Dictionary records the first use of the term 'sniper', meaning one who shoots at individuals from cover, in 1824. But the sniper, in practical military terms, was in business long before the term was adapted specifically to describe his activities.

Left: The modern sniper, as exemplified by this German on the Eastern Front, must possess patience and endurance, and also be well versed in the arts of concealment and fieldcraft.

According to legend, King Harold was shot dead by an enemy archer at the Battle of Hastings in 1066, so ending Saxon rule in England and introducing the continental feudal system into the country as Duke William of Normandy took over as king. Harold's death may have been one of the earliest recorded instances in European history of the sniper's art at work. The evidence is not entirely unambiguous. The Bayeux Tapestry can be seen as showing Harold with an arrow in his eye, but only three archers with shortbows are depicted on the Norman side, and one of those is mounted, pursuing retreating Saxons after the line was broken, late in the day on 21 October 1066.

Historian Sir Ralph Payne-Gallway was of the opinion that the Normans had crossbows by the time they invaded England, so perhaps the illustration of shortbows in the tapestry lends weight to the revisionist theory that it was woven in England, rather than in France, and that the shortbows depicted were an English interpretation of the unfamiliar weapons. The Saxons did have shortbows, but used them only for hunting. When it came to fighting, they wanted nothing between them and close action; for this reason they usually fought dismounted.

THE FIRST PROHIBITION

The popularity of crossbows on the battlefield increased as the weapon improved and became more effective. Then, in 1139, the Second Lateran Council prohibited it under penalty of an anathema – an official, church-sponsored curse – as a weapon hateful to God and unfit for Christians. It could still be used against infidels, of course.

The logic behind such a ban is worth thinking about, given modern moral queasiness about the use of snipers. The ostensible ground for banning the crossbow in European armies was the dreadful wounds it inflicted. But a soldier whom a shower of crossbow bolts missed still had to face heavy cavalry armed with lances, mace and chain, swords of various calibres, axes, or the morning-star club. Infantrymen had pole-arms – spear-length weapons

Above: The death of King Harold at Hastings was an early, if premature, example of the marksman's value in battle – hastening victory with a decisive blow to the enemy's leadership.

with a variety of metal heads that could skewer, slash or bash an opponent. Country men obliged to serve in their sovereigns' armies also pressed their own farm tools into service – slashing hooks, bill-hooks, flails, scythes, sickles, hammers, clubs, and other fierce implements.

However, there are two major differences between all these hack-and-slash weapons, which could cause really fearsome and usually fatal injuries, and the proscribed crossbow bolts. Put simply, crossbow bolts were indiscriminate. Their victims were not the losers in direct, hand-to-hand fighting. In this respect, crossbow archers had the same psychological effect on a medieval army as the sniper does on a modern fighting unit – absolutely no one on the battlefield could be certain that he might not be their victim.

Armed with crossbows, peasants could slaughter members of the nobility. And while that might be an unpleasant thought, a yet more unpleasant one was that if one's peasants picked off the cream of the opposition with crossbows before the chivalry could close with the enemy, there might be nobody of rank left to be taken hostage for ransom, and that would never do. Throughout most of history, the grassroots participants in war have agreed to be conscripted to do the nobility's dirty work because there was always the prospect of swag. Dip into Homer's *Iliad*, and this conclusion is immediately obvious. The Greeks didn't lay siege to Troy for 10 years just to get Helen back for Menelaus: they were there for whatever compensations they could lay hands on as the campaign progressed. Helen was just a cover story – the excuse, the moral justification. The medieval footsoldier likewise expected to have a share in the ransom of captured enemy nobles, and when battles were essentially an agglomeration of individual fights it was important that nobles should be spared as far as possible, not randomly wiped out by weapons like the crossbow.

So with that problem solved and a suitable cover-story in place, Christian armies were supposed to do without effective missile small arms when engaging

each other. They didn't, of course, and in 1199 King Richard I of England was shot and fatally wounded by a crossbowman defender of the castle of Chaluz, near Limoges in France. This was seen at the time as a judgement from Heaven for his permitting cross-bowmen into his army, although it can be seen 800 years later as an early example of the effectiveness of the lone sniper who takes out the enemy com-mander. But as long as the system of ransom remained as a sweetener to patriotic duty, the con-cept of sniping as we know it had no chance to develop.

British legends tell of the allegedly 'loveable' outlaw bowman Robin Hood, although he is often placed too early in history to have been a longbow-man. This weapon of yew wood was peculiar to Wales until after Edward I conquered the Principality in two campaigns between 1276 and 1283. The experiences of Edward Longshanks's army in those campaigns of being shot at, accurately and at con-siderable distances, led to the eventual employment of Welsh bowmen in any self-respecting British army thereafter. Apart from their effectiveness, longbows came with the bonus that the Lateran Council's threat of anathema didn't apply to them. But the British longbowmen, even at their most cel-ebrated victory – Agincourt (1415) – were not used as snipers in any modern sense: rather, they were used more as sharpshooters, and skirmishers were used in the British army after it had learned the lessons of the American War of Independence.

The mythical name of William Tell (fl. c. 1400) comes down to us as another early crossbow sniper, but for most of the Middle Ages the concept of sniping was on the back burner. Assassins worked close-in, with traditional daggers and poison as tools of their trade. In the 1500s armies adopted the new firelock guns, but landed themselves with something less effective than the bows that these early muskets replaced.

By 1588 the Spanish Armada was carrying more musketeers than bowmen to invade England, and bowmen feature not at all in the English Civil War

Above: Faced with the massed ranks of British Redcoats (as seen here at the Battle of Lexington 1775), the outnumbered American Revolutionaries soon adapted the techniques of hunting to pick off individual targets from cover.

(1642–9). Neither did snipers. The early matchlock muskets were smooth-bored and went off some time after the simple trigger caused the burning match to drop into the pan of black powder. This was not a weapon for precision shooting. Consequently, the army developed the concept of volley fire – everybody shooting at once into the massed ranks of the opposition. This system of controlling fire survived in British military thinking well into the twentieth century, some years after repeating rifles were issued to troops.

A better system of ignition, known as the wheel-lock, was developing alongside matchlock muskets, with the earliest examples dating from the early 1500s. However, these were expensive mechanical toys then, and gradually became accepted for target shooting, then hunting, eventually self-defence, and finally as weapons of war. By then, they were overtaken by cheaper and more reliable flintlock systems, which came into their own in the English Civil War.

THE AMERICAN RIFLEMAN

The situation in the New World was slightly different. Fledgling Americans found that they were in a big country where ranges to worthwhile suppers were much longer, and the chances of scraping together enough horses and dogs for a mounted hunt were fewer. The solution was found in the past, of course; archers had found ways of spinning their arrows around the axis of flight to improve their range and accuracy, and gunsmiths turned to finding ways of doing the same for bullets.

The system they came up with, in Pennsylvania in the early 1700s, was rifling. They cut a series of spiral grooves inside the barrel at the muzzle end. The soft lead ball was wrapped in a patch to make it a tight fit, and when the bullet was fired the impact of the blast caused a slight flattening of the ball at the side nearest the powder. This expanded the bullet's waistline slightly so that it was a tight fit to the bore,

Kentucky Rifle

Country of origin	USA	
Calibre	11.43mm	(.69 inches)
Overall length	1.52m	(60 inches)
Barrel length	1.12m	(44 inches)
Weight	3–4kg	(7–9lb)

• Stock and full-length fore-end in maple; sloping shoulder stock to curved butt, brass mount for shoulder; brass patchbox on right side of stock
• Full-length wooden ramrod in partially concealed track under barrel
• V rearsight notch and pin foresight
• Range up to 275m (300 yards) on the sights (longer shots can be 'aimed off')

Specifications vary according to period ('Kentucky' rifles date from the early 1700s to late in the percussion era, a century and a half later) but the data given here are typical.

The term 'Kentucky rifle' generically describes muzzle-loaded flintlock rifles, originally made in Pennsylvania by German gunsmiths, and then widely copied in the eighteenth century. Heinrich and Peter Leman were recorded as making fine flintlock rifles in 1732; in this period, the whole of the area between the Cumberland and Mississippi Rivers was known as 'Kentucky', and the name stuck to rifles suited to exploring and exploiting this wilderness. The name really stuck after the 'Kentucky Riflemen' – backwoods volunteers – were commemorated in song for their part in the Battle of New Orleans in 1812.

Loading the Kentucky rifle was a matter of pouring in a measure of loose powder, then putting a greased patch over the muzzle, adding the ball, then ramming the ball and patch home – an operation known as the 'patched-ball' system. The grease on the patch had the effect of cleaning the rifling as it went down, easing the seating of the ball. The military equivalent was to use paper cartridges, and to ram the greasy paper.

Ferguson Rifle

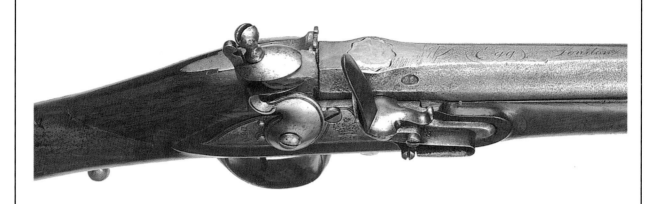

Country of origin	United Kingdom	
Calibre	14 bore	(17.27mm – .68 inches)
Overall length	1.2m	(47.25 inches)
Barrel length	80cm	(31.5 inches)
Weight	5kg	(11lb) not including bayonet

- Later models made in smaller bores
- Rifled with eight grooves
- No ramrod, small bayonet fitted in butt housing
- Articulated trigger to open breech for reloading

- Full-length walnut stock
- Peep rearsight, blade foresight
- Ordnance range tests at 182m (200 yards)

Patrick Ferguson, a retired captain of the 70th Foot, improved on work carried out by the Frenchman, Isaac de la Chaumette, to develop a breech-loaded flintlock rifle, which he successfully demonstrated to the Army Ordnance Board in April 1776. The following year he took command of 100 green-uniformed men armed with these rifles and served in the American colonies attached to the Hessian General Knyphausen's army group.

and when it reached the rifling grooves, it followed them and thus left the bore spinning on its own axis.

Done right, rifling makes a considerable difference to range and accuracy. The early American gunsmiths, who are usually said to have been Germans, found that a smaller bore and thus a lighter ball worked better for their customers' purposes. The weapons they made, despite originating in Pennsylvania, became known as Kentucky rifles. This generic term speaks of a long, sometimes octagonal barrel mounted with front and rear sights, a narrow bore, rifling, a graceful full-length stock and a brass patchbox on the opposite side to the cheek piece.

Original Kentucky rifles are now few, far between, and valuable, but many shootable reproductions are on the market. Italian models tend to be more faithful to the originals, while American makers tend to use the best of modern materials so as not to disadvantage their customers in any way during the limited 'primitive weapons' hunting season which precedes the deer hunt with modern weapons.

Loading a patch-and-ball weapon is slower than loading a musket, but when properly loaded, accuracy at distance can be achieved. One shot a minute from a Kentucky rifle would be good, but possible only from a fixed position with all the necessities laid out ready for use. The British army of the 1770s expected to get up to three shots per minute from each infantryman, and this rose to four a minute at the flintlock musket's zenith at Waterloo in 1815.

Original Kentucky barrels could be up to 1.5m (60 inches) long; bores were around 115mm (.45 inches), and the effective hunting range was practically as far as the shooter could see. To gauge the advantage this gave the eighteenth-century rifleman, one might note that a modern 12-bore shotgun firing No 6 shot is reckoned to be effective at up to only 32m (35 yards), and a wheel-lock, flint, or percussion smoothbore loaded with shot would not be any more effective than that.

Modern European riflemen, out deerstalking, look for a shot in the 90–140m (100–150-yard) bracket, and these flintlock rifles were easily capable of that. Americans tend to shoot over longer distances – it's a big country – than Europeans, and 275m (300-yard) hunting ranges are not uncommon. The twentieth-century handgun hunter Elmer Keith, who developed the .44-inch Magnum cartridge, claimed he could kill with his scoped revolver at up to 550m (600 yards). That might be optimistic for a man shooting a Kentucky rifle with open sights – for what can you see with the naked eye at that distance anyway? – but the weapon itself, as ever, was generally more accurate than its owner, and certainly capable of a lethal shot at such a distance.

The British found this out during the American War of Independence (1775–83). The British colonial authorities had earlier tried disarming the American militias, but the Americans hadn't played ball. They didn't fight fair either. Instead of lining up and trading volleys with British troops, they hid behind trees, picked their targets, and took them out, one at a time. In doing this, Americans were simply doing what they already knew – they adapted their hunting techniques to military service and performed effectively. They were a nation of snipers nearly half a century before the most respected British dictionary had a word for them.

The British reaction was almost unofficial, certainly low-key. Captain Patrick Ferguson was an

Above: A private of the 77th Foot presents his 'Brown Bess' flintlock musket. Variations on this rather inaccurate rifle were in use from the 1720s to the 1840s.

early developer of breech-loading technology, and the technique he developed allowed riflemen to load and fire faster than musket-bearing infantry. During trials in 1776 Ferguson let rip between four and seven shots a minute – a rate of fire nearly twice as fast as a smoothbore musket could shoot. The Ferguson rifle was reckoned by experts at the time to be one of the most deadly weapons in the British inventory, but the military diehards went only so far as to allow Ferguson to establish a unit of 100 men armed with his invention. Ferguson led them into action at the Battle of Brandywine Creek, where he was badly wounded. His corps of sharpshooters was disbanded, and his breech-loading rifles withdrawn from service. Ferguson recovered from his wounds but, ironically, was later killed on 7 October 1780 when a member of Colonel Daniel Morgan's Kentucky Riflemen shot him from about 410m (450 yards). As a result, Ferguson's unit surrendered; the loss forced the British to abandon their invasion of North Carolina.

Ferguson's second, no less ironic, claim to fame as a not-terribly-successful contributor to military history was his 'shot never taken'. Before the Battle of Brandywine Creek, Ferguson found himself in a position to make a shot on an unidentified American officer near Germantown, Pennsylvania. When the man turned away at a range of approximately 11.5m (25 yards), the honourable English officer could not bring himself to shoot his enemy in the back. The man Ferguson had in his sights was none other than General George Washington. 'Had Ferguson taken the shot,' one commentator wrote,

> one can assume that the entire history of what is today the United States would have been affected. Recall it was Washington who turned down the offer to be King of the Colonies after the successful resolution of the War for Independence. Had he not been in charge of the Colonial forces, not only would the outcome of the war have been in question, but so would the very nature of the Republic which rose from that conflict.

BIRTH OF THE GREENJACKETS

Otherwise, Britain followed the American sharp-shooting concept to the extent that after the loss of the American colonies a rifled musket design was commissioned and a rifle brigade formed to fight with these weapons. The Baker Rifle had a bore of similar diameter to the British musket and, courtesy of the rifling grooves, a somewhat longer range. The smoothbore 'Brown Bess' musket could be reasonably accurate at up to about 55m (60 yards) – which is uncomfortably close if you imagine an enemy formation that near. Musket balls could be effective at 90m (100 yards) and slightly more, but were inaccurate at that distance and beyond. Hence the British insistence on volley fire at massed enemy troops. Other European armies obligingly massed their troops – hence the British outrage at being picked off by backwoodsmen in buckskins who unsportingly refused, often as not, to fight in the open.

All projectiles slow down in flight, and spherical ball ammunition, once it dips below a certain velocity, tends to skitter or veer off its line of flight, so at up to around 75–85m (80–90 yards) from the muzzle the ball will be true but much lower than the point of aim. Beyond that distance, the veering action kicks in, so that the ball flies off line. This doesn't matter greatly when massed ranks of soldiers are firing at massed ranks of other soldiers, but for individual marksmanship, it's a disaster. The lesson of the American war was not entirely lost on British military chiefs. The rifle designed by London gunsmith Ezekiel Baker – and taken into British army service after winning a procurement competition in 1800 – dealt with this ballistic problem. Short-barrelled, capable of taking two sizes of shot (one that fit the rifling for long-range work, the other smaller and acting like a musket ball for close-in fighting), and fitted with a long sword bayonet, it was chosen primarily for its effectiveness at practical battlefield ranges, rather than for sniping as such.

Baker's tough and trustworthy rifle would have made an excellent arm for general issue to infantrymen, had the British military mind been flexible enough to adapt its battlefield tactics and train its troops to match the capability of the 'new' technology. Instead, the British raised a new regiment of the line, the 95th (to be dubbed the Rifle Brigade after the Battle of Waterloo), as a unit of sharpshooters who would support an advancing column of infantry. These 'skirmishers' operated, in rifleman Sir Harry Smith's words, 'in a cloud' in front of and on the flanks of the attacking columns, firing at long range to cause the enemy problems before the main bodies of troops engaged.

J.C. Barrett gives the background:

The [95th] Rifles were known by the moniker 'Greenjackets' because they wore distinctive green uniforms [an early, simple form of camouflage] that set them off from the other British infantry who wore jackets of fiery red ...

Historically, the soldiers chosen for service in the 95th Rifles were of the highest quality in their ability to handle firearms, their quick-thinking and their ferocious courage in combat. The Regiment was organized in a different fashion from most British Regiments of the time. Instead of fighting as one large unit, this elite corps was divided among many different Regiments in their Light Companies. The Light Companies were typically assigned duties such as scouting and advanced fighting (ahead of the main army). These 'thinking' soldiers proved to be amazingly valuable fighters.

The Baker Rifle

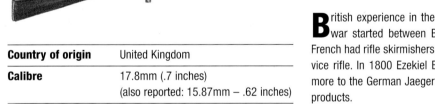

Country of origin	United Kingdom
Calibre	17.8mm (.7 inches) (also reported: 15.87mm – .62 inches)
Overall length	1.12m (44 inches)
Barrel length	76cm (30 inches)

• Seven-groove rifling
• Walnut stock with ramrod partially concealed and retained by two pipes in exposed section; patchbox fitted to right side of stock, but actually used for tools, as British riflemen issued with their ammunition in paper cartridge form didn't need separate patches
• V notch and blade sights
• Accurate at 92m (100 yards)

British experience in the Americas and the knowledge, when war started between Britain and France in 1793, that the French had rifle skirmishers, led to developmental work for a service rifle. In 1800 Ezekiel Baker's design was adopted. It owed more to the German Jaeger weapons than it did to the American products.

This rifle was also issued with a sword bayonet, a D-handled affair with a 61cm (24-inch) straight blade, which may have been more useful as a short sword than as a bayonet. A short carbine version was also issued to mounted units. This had a 48cm (19-inch) barrel and a captive swivel ramrod. No bayonet bar was fitted to carbines, as mounted troops had swords.

The Baker was replaced in service in 1837 by the Brunswick rifle, a larger-bored, two-groove rifled percussion weapon, which was unpopular because the grooves quickly fouled and made the weapon difficult to load. The ball had a raised rib around its diameter, which engaged the two deep rifling grooves for loading. Once these grooves were dirty, the ball couldn't be seated.

In effect, these were snipers who did not take the trouble to hide, and they fought as a unit, not as lone killers. The 95th first achieved fame and glory in the Peninsular War against Napoleon.

There were nonetheless instances of what we would now recognise as classic sniper actions. During the retreat to Corunna in 1808, Tom Plunkett of the 95th felled French General Colbert at the bridge of Cacabelos with one shot; while at the siege of Badajos in 1812, a band of riflemen – 'forty as prime fellows as ever pulled the trigger' according to eyewitness George Simmons – silenced a battery of French guns. But the following two passages from Harry Smith's autobiography show how the 95th more habitually fought. At the Battle of Sabugal in 1811, he wrote (with typical forthrightness):

Sir W[illiam]. Erskine commanded the cavalry and Light Division, a near-sighted old ass, and we got méléed with Reynier's *corps d'armée* strongly posted on heights above Sabugal, and attacked when the Duke [of Wellington – then in fact still Sir Arthur Wellesley] intended we should have moved round their left to Quadraseyes, as the 5th, 4th, and 3rd Divisions were to attack their front in the centre of their position. However, we began, and never was more gallantry mutually displayed by friend and foe than on this occasion, particularly by dear old Beckwith and his 1st Brigade. Some guns were taken and retaken several times. A French officer on a grey horse was most gallant. Old Beckwith, in a voice like thunder, roared out to the Riflemen, 'Shoot that fellow, will you?' In a moment he and his horse were knocked over, and Sydney exclaimed, 'Alas! you were a noble fellow.'

Two years later, Smith tells, at the Battle of Vittoria, the 95th

were hotly engaged all the afternoon pursuing the French over very broad ditches. Until we neared Vittoria to our left, there was a plain free from ditches. The confusion of baggage, etc., was indescribable. Our Brigade was moving rapidly on, when such a swarm of French Cavalry rushed out from among the baggage into our skirmishers, opposite a company of the 2nd Battalion Rifle Brigade, commanded by Lieutenant Tom Cochrane, we thought they must have been swept off. Fortunately for Tom, a little rough ground and a bank enabled him to command his Company to lie down, and such a reception they gave the horsemen, while some of our Company were flying to their support, that the French fled with a severe loss. Our Riflemen were beautiful shots, and as undaunted as bulldogs. We knew so well, too, how to support each other, that scarcely had the French Dragoons shown themselves when Cochrane's rear was supported, and we had such mutual confidence in this support that we never calculated on disaster, but assumed the boldest front and bearing.

THE FULL NELSON

The British had had a hefty hint of the value of the solitary marksman well before the death of Colbert, and the reaction of most generals on the battlefield indicates how comprehensively they failed to learn the lesson. After Waterloo, Harry Smith fumed (he had an infamous temper) that successful skirmishing tactics learned from experience were thrown away in favour of aping German troop deployments.

Even at sea a memorable shot by an enemy sniper produced a peculiar response. In October 1805 the combined fleets of France and Spain left the safety of Cadiz harbour and were promptly pounced on by the Royal Navy in a two-pronged formation. Standing on the quarter-deck of HMS *Victory*, the lead ship in the left-hand column, Admiral Lord Nelson was shot by a sniper lodged in the rigging of the French ship *Redoubtable*. The weapon used was the standard French musket of the day, and the range was probably no more than 75m (82 yards), but this

Above: Admiral Horatio Nelson is perhaps the most famous victim of a sniper. His death prompted development of the first dedicated counter-sniping weapon – the seven-barrelled Nock Volley Gun, issued for sailors to blast snipers from the rigging of warships.

was probably no more than 75m (82 yards), but this shot echoes that of the crossbowman who got Richard Lionheart in 1199.

At Trafalgar, Nelson's death did not affect the outcome of the battle. He had planned the operation, set his fleet on its course, clearly instructed close action, and could then have had no further influence on the battle. Lord Montgomery, who commanded British troops in World War II, said that he had never seen a plan of battle survive contact with the enemy: he did his bit as a general, and then it was up to the troops and their commanders to improvise, survive and prevail. Nelson's fleet was in just this position as he lay dying in the *Victory*'s cockpit.

Britain's response to the death of their national hero was curious. The navy didn't get snipers of their own, which modern hindsight suggests might

Enfield P53

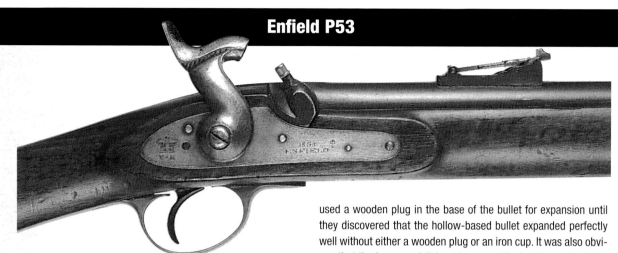

Country of origin	United Kingdom
Calibre	14.65mm (.577 inches)
Overall length	1.21m (47.5 inches)
Barrel length	85cm (33.5 inches)
Weight	5kg (11lb)

• Pritchett base-cavity bullet in paper cartridge
• Three-groove rifling
• Barrel secured by three wrap-around barrel bands
• Full-length walnut stock; iron ramrod in groove underneath
• Blade foresight; adjustable rearsight to 730m (800 yards), but at that distance the tip of the foresight looks about 2.5m (8ft) wide
• Manufactured at the Royal Small Arms Factory, Enfield, and by private contractors

The British Ordnance Board sought, in the late 1840s, to combine the available technology of percussion locks and rifled barrels, to produce one weapon for all troops. In 1849, Captain Claude-Étienne Minié had patented a bullet that seemed to solve the loading problem. It was a hollow-based elongated bullet, rather than a ball, with an iron cup fitted to the hollow base. The theory was that the bullet could be smaller than the bore, for ease of loading, and that when fired, the iron cup would be thrust forwards into the softer lead bullet, causing the latter to expand and fill the bore.

The British adopted this idea as the P51 rifle-musket, bore of 17.83mm (.702 inches) with four rifling grooves. However, they used a wooden plug in the base of the bullet for expansion until they discovered that the hollow-based bullet expanded perfectly well without either a wooden plug or an iron cup. It was also obvious that the bore needn't be a large as .7in, but the main obstacle to reducing it was the Duke of Wellington, who required that the projectile should weigh at least an ounce (28.35g). His death in 1852 paved the way for a logical bore reduction for the Enfield P53 rifle-musket – the most significant advance in weapons technology ever in one leap.

Colonel Samuel Colt rates a mention at this point. He had visited London in 1851 to exhibit at the Great Exhibition of that year, and stayed on to open a London factory to make his revolving pistol. He also gave evidence to the government enquiry of the day, and advised them on the mechanical principles of mass production, which was the only thing he really invented.

SNIDER

Tests and trials of breech-loading systems kept the British busy after the Indian mutiny, and by 1864 Jacob Snider's system had been adopted. This was a conversion of the P53 rifle musket into a breechloader by way of a hinged breech-block. A small catch on the left side permitted the block to hinge to the right, where it could be pulled rearwards to expend the cartridge case from the breech. The new round was then loaded, breech closed and the hammer cocked for the next shot. The hammer engaged a primer on the base of the cartridge case by way of a firing pin which ran right through the breech-block.

Conversions started in 1864 and the data for the Snider is thus exactly the same as for the P53 Enfield. The breech-block conversion is readily apparent, with conversion details struck on the left side of the wrist. Original markings can still be seen on the lockplate, so an examination shows the date when the rifle was originally manufactured as an Enfield on the lock, with the conversion date on the wrist.

Gun. This seven-barrelled weapon was designed to clear enemy rigging, but more as a shotgun would, firing all barrels simultaneously. Nelson's way to clear enemy rigging would have been to shoot the masts off with cannon – gaudy, but effective. Still, something had to be seen to be done, and the solution was a piece of kit that called for no specialist training. The Nock Volley Gun stands in history as one of the more bizarre weapons specifically intended for shooting enemies. It did not last long in service as, after Napoleon's final defeat in 1815, Britain had no serious maritime enemies for several decades.

Few Nock Volley Guns survive, but you can see one being fired by Richard Widmark, playing Jim Bowie, in the 1960 film *The Alamo*. There's no apparent historical authority for this scene. Bowie's only known weapon (apart from his famous knife) is now preserved in the Texas Rangers Hall of Fame Museum in Waco, Texas. It was a rifle, allegedly taken from his body in the hospital at the Alamo when the buildings were stormed early in the morning of the 6th March 1836. It is a .36in calibre (100 bore) pea rifle, which was an excellent short-range sniping weapon or small-game rifle, and is an altogether more likely item for Bowie to employ.

Nearly half a century after Nelson's death, the British army started to receive rifle muskets on issue. The Enfield P53 was a .577in (24 bore) muzzle-loaded rifle with an effective range of up to half a mile. This increase in effectiveness by a factor of 10 represents the greatest single leap in small arms technology the British army has ever had. Technically, every soldier could now be a sniper. Enemy troops could no longer form up close enough to a British formation to shout insults across the divide without being fired on. The first to discover this were the Russians, when they engaged British troops in the Crimean campaign (1854–6). The P53 rifle musket does not seem to have been used to its full advantage, however, as the troops were led by men who thought that volley fire and bayonet charges were still the way to do things. The lessons of the Peninsular War had long been forgotten.

Above: General John Sedgwick became famous for his last words: 'They couldn't hit an elephant at this dist…!' He was one of several senior Union officers killed by shots from the unreliable but accurate Whitworth rifle.

Quantities of P53 rifles were exported from Britain, with buyers including the Confederate States of America, who on secession from the Union in 1861 found themselves very short on military hardware. Ships delivering small arms had to run a blockade mounted by the Federal North.

Sniper shots became a feature of the American Civil War, although snipers were still thought of as skirmishers, generally acting in concert to harass the enemy's massed troops, and to pick off officers and cannon crews, rather than as solitary, secretive killers of high-value targets. But there were exceptions. A Confederate sniper killed Major General John F. Reynolds on 1 July 1863 at Gettysburg; he was the senior commander on the field at the time, and the ultimate the result of that shot was the loss

Above: A rebel sharpshooter picks off a Union sentry during the Civil War. The usually outnumbered Confederates relied more heavily on the individual marksman, but by late in the war snipers of both sides were using telescopic sights and concealment techniques.

of the town by the Union army. A few weeks later, on 19 September 1863, a Confederate sniper armed with a British Whitworth .45in muzzle-loading percussion rifle, shooting a 530-grain bullet, mortally wounded Union General William H. Lytle during the Battle of Chicamauga. Lytle was leading a charge at the time, and died the following day.

The American Civil War also produced some of the most famously ironic of 'famous last words' ever spoken, when Union army General John Sedgwick was killed at the Battle of Spotsylvania on 9 May

1864. Sedgwick saw his men dodging at the sound of Confederate bullets, and jovially shouted: 'What! What! Men, dodging this way for single bullets! ... I am ashamed of you. They couldn't hit an elephant at this dist…!'

Below: 'A Sharpshooter's Last Sleep' is the title of this poignant photograph taken by Alexander Gardener immediately after the Battle of Gettysburg, July 1863.

His words were cut short by a bullet drilling him through the head. A Sergeant Grace, of the 4th Georgia Infantry, had fired the shot from a Whitworth target rifle; the distance so rashly mocked by Sedgwick was about 730m (800 yards). An eyewitness nearby described later how Sedgwick's face 'turned slowly to me, the blood spurting from his left cheek under the eye in a steady stream. He fell in my direction; I was so close

The race to repeaters

In principle, turning-bolt rifles are all the same. In the locked position the bolt holds the breech shut and presents the firing pin to the round's primer. The bolt is released by an upwards movement to unlock the lugs, then is pulled back. The bolt-head includes an extractor, which pulls the empty case clear. Once clear of the chamber, the case is thrown clear by an ejector boot, the next round, or the magazine follower. The fresh round is then chambered as the bolt is closed, while the striker is left cocked ready for firing.

Several countries researched their repeating rifle options, but the various systems went round Europe like this:

1884

Germany adopts a repeating variant of their M1871 single-shot bolt-action rifle (itself an improvement of the earlier needle-fire rifle), designated the M1871/84. This has a tubular magazine under the barrel which can hold 10 rounds, and a magazine cut-off, so that the rifle can be used as a single-shot weapon until the cut-off is released and the ammunition in the magazine can be fed.

1886

France, which had a single-shot bolt-action rifle in 1866 – the Chassepot, improved in 1874 as the Gras – adopts the M1886 Lebel rifle. This also has a tube magazine under the barrel and a magazine cut-off, but its innovation is the use of a nitro-cellulose based 'smokeless' powder. This enables the French to reduce the bore from an average of 10–11mm (.39–.44 inches) to just 8mm (.32 inches). This might not sound like much, but ammunition is the heaviest component of any weapons system and calibre reductions have progressively increased the number of rounds of ammunition individual soldiers can carry.

1888

Germany goes for the 'Commission' Mauser; a five-shot, clip-fed, smokeless, 8mm (.32-inch) repeater. Britain adopts the eight-shot Lee Metford, with 7.7mm (.303-inch) calibre, using compressed black-powder pellets.

1889

Belgium buys the right to make the Mauser under contract, and forms a company (Fabrique Nationale des Armes de Guerre, or FN for short) to make it. FN improve the design, which is adopted as the M1889 by Belgium. It also becomes the first military bolt-action repeating rifle to go on sale to the general public (Belgium is a small country with a small army, and FN needs the extra income provided by commercial sales).

1891

Russia adopts a commercial design, the Mosin Nagant as the M1891, in 7.62 x 54mm (0.3 x 2.1 inches) rimmed. Their design is clip-loaded, like the Mausers and holds five rounds in the magazine. The Italians adopt the Mannlicher-Carcano, another turning-bolt system. With this one, six rounds of 6.6mm (.25-inch) ammunition are held in a clip, which is loaded into the rifle where a spring feeds the rounds. With the last round gone, the insertion of a new clip from above pushes the empty clip out of the bottom.

1892

The Americans buy in a bolt-action design – the Krag-Jorgenson from Norway – and adopt it as the M1892 .30/40 Krag. The world ignores the Americans and rapidly divides into Mauser users and the rest. The British Lee Metford is upgraded to take a 10-shot detachable box magazine, and is converted for smokeless ammunition in 1895. This rifle is designated the Lee Enfield Mk 1.

1898

The Mauser design reaches its zenith and is progressively adopted by more independent countries than any other weapon of the era. The Americans come to realise what a poor weapon the Krag is and, in the search for a twentieth-century weapons system, finally arrive at the M1903 Springfield.

Above: During the Boer War, both sides used long-range repeating rifles; but the Boers were self-trained game hunters, and often had the advantage when they held the high ground, as here at Spion Kop.

him that my effort to support him failed and I fell with him.' Sedgwick's death delayed the advance of the Union troops and contributed to the Confederate General Robert E. Lee's victory.

It was during the American Civil War that snipers – then called sharpshooters – first proved how well-aimed fire at individual targets could destroy the effectiveness of whole units. In consequence sharpshooters were singularly hated by line troops on both sides of the conflict, and the tradition was born of showing no mercy to them when they were caught. The degree of feeling aroused is illustrated by this anecdote:

At Yorktown, during the Peninsular Campaign of 1862, Private John Ide of the 1st Regiment engaged in a battle with a Confederate sharpshooter at long range. Armed with a telescopic target rifle, Ide was firing from the side of an old out-house, exchanging several shots with his adversary. Soldiers from both sides looked on with interest as the duel progressed. When Ide

Martini Henry

Barrel length	74.93cm	(29 1/2 inches)
Weight (long butt)	4.14kg	(9lb 2oz)

Country of origin	United Kingdom
Calibre	14.65/11.43mm (.577/450-inch) bottleneck
Overall length	1.26m	(49 3/4 inches)

• Wooden shoulder stock, fitted to socket on rear of receiver and available in two lengths; fore-end wood in one piece, fitted under barrel by two bands
• Front blade sight; rear ladder sight, graduated for 914m (1000 yards)

brought up his rifle to fire again, he suddenly spun round, hit by a Confederate bullet square in his forehead. The great shout of triumph from the enemy lines only served to remind [Union sharpshooters] of the dangers of their calling.

The Confederate army relied heavily on such marksmen – most of whom had grown up with a rifle in their hands, hunting, out of necessity, for the pot – to compensate for the lack of heavy weapons and plain numbers of infantry available. The rebel sharp-shooters were adept at harrying Union troops and making artillery units ineffective, but specialised in taking out Union officers. Unfortunately for the Confederacy, these sharpshooters were neither numerous nor quite effective enough to stem the tide of the well-equipped and more voluminous Union forces.

After the war of mutual destruction, the American army had little use for snipers, however, as they had only Indians to fight – and that enemy always sought close action when they offered battle at all. The 5th Cavalry went West to bring 'peace' to the Frontier, disposing of their repeating Spencers and re-equip-ping with single-shot Springfields. The development

of long-range hunting rifles was left to the civilian market.

DUTCH AFRICAN LESSONS

Between the American Civil War and the end of nineteenth century, rifle and ammunition technology developed dramatically. The percussion cap (which had succeeded the flintlock in the late eighteenth century, to make firearms weatherproof) had been a huge advance, but with few exceptions it was applied to muzzle-loading weapons. Breech-load-ers, using linen or paper cartridges, still demanded the separate insertion of ball, powder, and cap before being fired. By the 1870s, the modern car-tridge had appeared. The bullet was wedged into a cylindrical metal case on top of the powder, which in turn was ignited by a hammer striking a percus-sion cap that was integral to the cartridge. Gunpowder was replaced with smokeless 'nitro' propellants, so that soldiers firing volleys no longer had their aim almost immediately obscured by clouds of white smoke – and individual snipers could be detected by no more than the transient flash from their muzzles. The next logical development from the self-contained cartridge was magazine-fed 'repeating' rifles. Among the first were the famous

Winchester '73, seen in virtually every Hollywood Western ever made, which carried rounds in a tube fixed under the barrel, and jacked them into the chamber by the lever action of an extended trigger guard. Then, the American James P. Lee and the German Ferdinand von Mannlicher independently invented the box magazine. This was detachable from the rifle, so plenty of pre-loaded magazines could be carried – and rapidly fed into the rifle – by infantrymen. Greater understanding of metallurgy and the physics of what happened inside a rifle barrel when a round was fired were all fed into firearms production. The next result was the availability of relatively inexpensive rifles of unprecedented accuracy, durability and rate of fire.

It was in South Africa, as the nineteenth century closed, that this new technology was proven – and where British troops were once again taught what they had unfortunately forgotten after the American War of Independence. This time their enemy were Boers – fiercely independent men of Dutch extraction who had begun settling the interior of South Africa two centuries before in order to farm out of reach of bureaucratic governments. These farmer-hunters, when confronted by the might of the British army, formed themselves into 'Kommandos' – mounted infantry units – and rode off to battle. Their 8mm Mauser rifles were capable of accurate fire at up to about 1100m (1200 yards), and volley fire from them was effective at nigh on twice that distance.

British rifles were also effective now at long ranges; Britain had adopted the Lee Metford in 1889 as a replacement for the inadequate Martini Henry. The first model had a magazine of eight rounds and fired a .303in bullet using compressed black powder. By the time of the Second Boer War in 1899, the newer model Lee Enfield took 10 rounds in the magazine, and used an early smokeless powder. The rear sights on these rifles went to more than 1800m (up to 2000 yards), and the long-range sights on the left hand side went to more than 3100m (up to 3400 yards), or more than 3km (almost 2 miles).

The difference between the British and the Boers was that the latter had practised on game at long range and knew the effectiveness of their rifles. Hiding on hill tops overlooking advancing British formations, they took their pick of targets. The British could not see where to return fire, as the Boer ammunition was smokeless, and in action after action and battle after battle British losses to these riflemen were excessive. Embarrassment, patriotism, and shame had their effect. Charitable gifts were made to Britain's National Rifle Association to ensure that civilian and military marksmen could practise shooting at moving targets. After the war, Lord Roberts, the field marshal who had commanded British troops in South Africa, lent his name to a (generally successful) campaign to encourage rifle shooting among working men, in the hope of creating a nation of marksmen 'with a rifle in every cottage'. The lesson was not learned, however, that individual riflemen can make a critical difference on the battlefield. The Aldershot system insisted on training soldiers, no matter how good they were individually, to fire en masse at massed bodies of enemy.

The British search for a custom-made breechloader managed to avoid the widely acclaimed Remington Rolling Block and led instead, in 1872, to this, with a barrel designed by Alexander Henry and with a Henry Peabody action as improved by Frederick von Martini. The action was too short for the chosen cartridge, so the round had to be redesigned to fit the available space which led to the first bottle-neck round – a 14.65mm (.577-inch) Snider case, necked down to 11.43mm (.45 inches) at the mouth. This gave enough interior space for the required charge in a round short enough to cope with the Martini action.

In this, the trigger guard also acted as an under-lever which, when depressed, dropped the breech-block. This action was also supposed to clear any cartridge or case in the chamber, and actually would if the gun was cool and clean; otherwise the case only emerged halfway and had to be prised out, usually with a penknife.

Once clear, the chamber could be reloaded with a fresh round. The action was cocked automatically on opening, so the next round could be fired as soon as the action was closed. In tests, we managed eight rounds in a minute from a Martini Henry. It sounds impressive, but not when compared to how fast a Zulu can run. An Olympic-class athlete can make 90m (100 yards) on a track in less than 10 seconds, so if you allow a Zulu on open ground 30 seconds for the same distance, you get, at the very best, four shots off before he reaches you with his assegai. The only plus to this scenario is that if he's coming straight at you, there's no lead.

Staff at the Woolwich Arsenal managed 20 rounds in a minute in their tests, which led to the weapon's adoption. In reality, ejection of spent cases was a nightmare, particularly as weapons heated up or became dirty. The action would pull the case about half-clear, and soldiers tended to stab the soft rolled brass case with a penknife to strip it from the breech. Various attempts were made to solve this problem, which was caused by the shape of the breech, a curved ramp on which the case was supposed to slide rearwards and up. The Mark 4, in 1886, had an extended underlever to try to increase leverage, but nothing worked on the .577/450-inch cartridge.

The tests may have been conducted when the proposed cartridge was a longer tapering-cased .45 inches, similar in appearance to the .45/70. In any case, the British army was stuck with this white

Right: The main British rifle in the latter part of World War II was the Lee Enfield No 4 Mark 1, seen here in its conventional form with troops in Holland in January 1945. This model was the basis of the main sniper rifle used by the UK in the war, the Mark 1(T).

Lee Enfield

Country of origin	United Kingdom
Calibre	7.69mm (.303 inches)
Overall length	1.19m (47 inches)
Barrel length	76.2cm (30 inches)
Weight	4.3kg (9lb 8oz)

• Wooden shoulder stock bolted to socket in rear of receiver; separate fore-end woodwork held in place by barrel bands and a nose cap; detachable wooden top handguard behind rear sight

• Front barleycorn sight; rear ladder adjustable to 1830m (2000 yards), side-mounted volley sights adjustable to 3108m (3400 yards)
• Turning-bolt operating system; single-lug locking
• Detachable 10-round box magazine; clip-fed top-loading after 1908; cut-off on rifle body (weapons up to 1916) for use as a single-shot weapon
• Accurate shooting at a 61cm (24-inch) bull possible at 1100m (1200 yards)
• Long Lee and SMLE rifles made in the UK by the Royal Small Arms Factory, Enfield, and private contractors; SMLE rifles also made, with slight variations, at Ishapore Arsenal in India, and Lithgow in Australia; No4 Mk1 rifles all made in the USA and Canada

elephant until the Lee Metford came along. After 1888, these rifles and carbines were downgraded to reserve or surplus; many were converted to .303-inch Metford or Enfield, and this cartridge did eject reasonably well. Many more were converted to .22-inch rimfire for the Workingmen's Society of Miniature Rifle Clubs and cadet corps throughout Britain.

The Lee Metford/Enfield rifle of the Boer War gave way in 1903 to the Short Magazine Lee Enfield (SMLE, or 'Smelly' to the Tommies). Its design arose out of other lessons learned during the Boer War and was issued to all branches of the service. Up to this point infantrymen had longer barrelled rifles while cavalry, artillery and engineers carried shorter carbines. The difference in the Boer War was a 76cm (30-inch) barrel for the infantry and a 46cm (18-inch) barrel for carbine troops, and a corresponding loss of accuracy for the latter.

Below: Soldiers of the 1st Cameron Regiment use binoculars to scout for a German sniper in an area called the 'Cabbage Patch', France, November 1914. The depth of the trench and the survival of the crops is typical of the early war period.

The Lee Enfield rifle was modified extensively between 1895 and the early 1950s when, in its No4 form, it was finally replaced in British service by the 7.62mm (.3-inch) L1A1 self-loading rifle.

In 1903 the barrel was reduced by 15cm (6 inches) to make the Short Magazine Lee Enfield (SMLE), which replaced both the rifle and carbine in service. An additional top handguard was provided to fully enclose the barrel. This weapon, and remaining Long Lees and carbines, were upgraded in 1908 with a clip-loading system, in which the clip was discarded as the rounds were pressed into the magazine. This necessitated fitting a bridge charger guide over the bolt track.

The magazine cut-off was not usually fitted to rifles made after 1916. The SMLE was designated Rifle No1 and ran to three Marks as issued. The Mark 4 was produced only as a prototype. A Mark 5 went to troop trials in the 1920s. These were essentially the same as earlier models, but the rear sight is fitted behind the bridge charger guide instead of on the barrel.

The author has engaged and sunk a floating 205l (45-gallon) oil drum with a short-model Lee Enfield at 1830m (2000 yards). The M1912 Vickers tripod-mounted machine gun, which used the same ammunition, had sights to 3658m (4000 yards), but if you lie in the long grass to avoid incoming fire you can't see more than about 90m (100 yards) and at that range if you can see it, you can hit it.

During World War II a new variant was produced as the No4 Mark 1 (No1 being the SMLE, No2 the Long Lee, No3 the P14). This was the result of various trials and tests. Still a .303-inch rifle, the rear sight was behind the bridge charger guide, the fore-sight was proud of the fore-end woodwork, and the bayonet was mounted on barrel lugs instead of the underlug of the SMLE. SMLE rifles were used throughout World War II in North Africa, the Far East, Sicily and Italy. The No4 rifles put in a late appearance. Their first use in action seems to have been at Dieppe in 1942, and they saw extensive use on D Day and thereafter.

The first British sniping rifle of the twentieth century was a No1 Mk3 rifle fitted with Lattey optical sights which clipped to the fore-end and rear sight to make a primitive telescope. Other No1 Mk3 rifles were modified with the addition of telescopic sights by the Periscope Prism Co or Aldis Brothers on mounts designed to be fitted to the rifles.

The World War II sniper variants, designated No4 Mk1(T), were superior examples of the No4 Mk1 selected from standard production lines, with a wooden cheekpiece fitted atop the shoulder stock, and a No32 telescopic sight on a Holland & Holland mount. The short-range accuracy – meeting a requirement of a 75mm (3-inch) group at 92m (100 yards) – is nothing special, but the rifles get more accurate the further you go out. Introduced in 1942, they served superbly throughout the rest of World War II and served up to 1991 as the L42A1, a slightly modified version.

The difference also called for different ammunition: the standard infantry .303 round contained enough powder to push a bullet along 76cm (30 inches) of pipe, but less was needed to push the same bullet out of a 46cm (18-inch) barrel. The logistical advantages of issuing one type of ammunition are obvious; and that was the only real practical lesson the British learned in the Boer War.

The British army thought that machine guns would have dealt with the Boers, so in the comparative peace of the Edwardian era, several attempts were made to increase the number of machine guns available to the army. These efforts failed, and so the army school of musketry at Hythe, Kent, devised what became known as 'mad minute musketry' to compensate. This involved troops firing up to 30 aimed shots in a minute, and was achieved by a combination of the new clip loading system for the rifle magazines, a rapid, smooth bolt action, and by using the third finger on the trigger, leaving the index finger poised to lift the bolt as soon as the shot had been fired.

The idea was to create a 'beaten zone' – an area that was so thoroughly invested with British bullets

Gewehr 1898

- Front blade sights, rear ramp to 2000m (2190 yards)
- Turning-bolt operating system
- Integral five-round top-loaded magazine

Country of origin	Germany	
Calibre	7.92 x 57mm	(.312 x 2.25 inches)
Overall length	1.26m	(49 1/2 inches)
Barrel length	74.3cm	(29 1/4 inches)
Weight	4.2kg	(9lb 4oz)

- One-piece stock and fore-end; separate over-barrel fore-end in wood, secured by one barrel band and a nose cap

The rifle was modified in the 1930s. The barrel was shortened to 60cm (23.6 inches) and the bolt head turned down. The intention was one rifle for all branches of service instead of issuing rifles to infantry and carbines to other units. Had World War II not intervened, this rifle would have replaced the G98 and some carbines, while the rest of the carbines would have been replaced by machine pistols. As it turned out, Germany, like Britain, had to use World War I rifles throughout World War II.

that nobody in that killing ground could survive. It was a nice theory and, like the anti-aircraft box barrage of World War II, it was ultimately ineffective.

A RIFLEMAN'S WAR

When hostilities broke out between Britain and Germany in August 1914, the accurate, rapid fire from regular British soldiers of the expeditionary force – the 'Contemptible Little Army' – was taken for machine-gun fire and helped to stop the advance of the German conscript army of three million men. Then the war bogged down in trenches extending from the North Sea to Switzerland. With conventional ideas of warfare resulting in a stalemate, innovations were sought.

There was no shortage of them in the 1914–18 war: among them were aircraft, tanks, poison gas, hand grenades – and snipers. Regular officers with experience in the Boer War knew that good rifle-

men, operating singly, in pairs or small groups, could, in directing their rifle fire properly, have an effect on regular soldiers that was disproportionate to their numbers. The fieldcraft of the Boers was learned while hunting, and Britain was, by this time, blessed with no shortage of men with such fieldcraft experience: deerstalkers.

Enter Lord Lovat. Of Highland noble stock, an officer, gentleman, and a deerstalker, he raised a regiment, the Lovat Scouts, from the Highland estates where the same kind of skills that the Boers had developed on the Veld were equally finely tuned for the pursuit of deer. These men were not designated snipers. They were scouts, observers – men who could hide up with a good telescope and watch the enemy and interpret his movements, as had the Boers. But their value as marksmen and trainers of marksmen had yet to be fully realised.

The German army, on the other hand, divined the value of sniping almost as soon as the stalemate of the trenches set in. British intelligence officers soon became aware of the number of head and chest injuries caused by German rifle fire. It seemed that the Germans were systematically sniping at the British trenches to good effect. The fact was that the Duke of Ratibor had commandeered many thousands of sporting rifles with telescopic sights and had put them into the hands of experienced foresters, moving them forwards as hunting units. These men also carried specially developed SmK ammunition that was more accurate than the stan-

Below: German storm troops are seen practising an attack near Sedan, May 1917. Stick grenades were the preferred assault weapon, but in periods when the line was static, the German sniper earned a fearsome reputation.

dard infantry issue. Also on offer to German marksmen was the accurized version of the issue 7.92mm Gewehr 1898 (Gew 98) rifle, adapted for use with telescopic sights, in which Germany was the world leader at the time.

By 1915 the Germans had a system in place. Their instruction manual for using the SmK round stated:

> The weapons with telescopic sights are very accurate up to 300 metres [330 yards]. They must be issued only to qualified marksmen who can assure results when firing from trench to trench,

Above: Supported by a regular infantryman with a rifle and Panzerfaust anti-tank weapon, an SS sniper looks out from his hide. The sniper is usually portrayed as the 'Lone Wolf', but the benefits of a two-man sniper/observer team have been recognised.

and especially at dusk or during clear nights when ordinary weapons are not satisfactory.

Perhaps the most important passage in the manual read as follows:

> Marksmen are not limited to the location of their unit, and are free to move anywhere they can see a

valuable target ... The marksman will use his telescope to watch the enemy front, recording his observations in a notebook, as well as his cartridge consumption and probable results of his shots.

Marksmen are exempted from additional duty. They will wear a special badge of two crossed oak leaves above the upper badge of the cap.

If anyone 'invented' the sniper as we know him today, it was the German imperial army of World War I.

To counter this threat, men with hunting experience had to devise counter-sniper techniques and then get sniper units active in the British army. Along with Lovat and his ghillies, Major Hesketh-Prichard and his colleague Captain Gaythorn-Hardy, Colonel Lanford-Lloyd and Captain Owen Underhill are remembered today as the prime movers in developing British sniping. Again, it was from the ranks of peacetime hunters that many of the first snipers were drawn; men who already had the fieldcraft and the shooting skills could be trained more quickly. Deerstalker J.K. Forbes wrote:

Quite a number of half-forgotten and much neglected faculties of mine seem to be coming all into use again, all those years of working with maps and wandering in Scottish wildernesses, and the faculty of looking into things through a pair of glasses, and the faculty of being able to use all these quite decently when a big strain is on your nerves, when you must either raise your head into danger or the information be lost. [*Student and Sniper Sergeant: A Memoir of J.K. Forbes*, ed. by William Taylor and Peter Diak (Hodder and Stoughton, 1916)]

The British, and the Canadians in particular, took the sniping war to the enemy. After a year of trench warfare, Hesketh-Prichard noted,

... the Germans were just beginning to be a little shy of our snipers on those fronts to which organisation had penetrated, and it was clear that the time would arrive when careful Hans and conscientious Fritz would come very troglodytic, as indeed they did. We had, therefore, turned our minds to think out plans and ruses by which the enemy might be persuaded to give us a target.

K98K

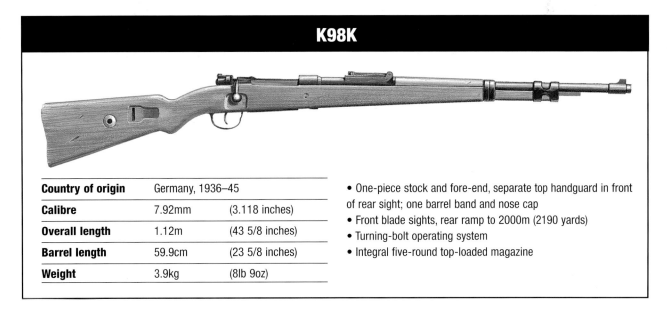

Country of origin	Germany, 1936–45	
Calibre	7.92mm	(3.118 inches)
Overall length	1.12m	(43 5/8 inches)
Barrel length	59.9cm	(23 5/8 inches)
Weight	3.9kg	(8lb 9oz)

- One-piece stock and fore-end, separate top handguard in front of rear sight; one barrel band and nose cap
- Front blade sights, rear ramp to 2000m (2190 yards)
- Turning-bolt operating system
- Integral five-round top-loaded magazine

Left: On the Eastern front, each side had a healthy respect for the other's snipers. On the Russian side, they were not necessarily all men. Maria Lalkova, a soldier in the Czechoslovak exile army, was credited with 'dozens of dead Nazis'.

The basis of all these 'ruses' was essentially the same: to lure enemy snipers into giving away their positions by exposing dummy heads (or even whole 'bodies') or appearing to be an incompetent and so drawing fire, and so on, and then responding with deadly accurate fire from several prepared snipers.

The first British sniping rifle was a Short Lee Enfield Mark III fitted with simple optical sights. These were two optics, fitted to the front and rear sights. They worked on the Galilean principle to form a telescope. Three designs were approved by the War Office, by Lattey, Neill and Martin. Others were available as private purchases (no licensing restrictions applied then).

Among the American expeditionary force, which began to join the war in 1917, was Company G, 328th Infantry Regiment, 82nd Division, known as the All-American Division because it was contained men from every state in the Union. Company G arrived on the Western Front in France on 27 June 1918. In it was Alvin York, a 30-year-old backwoodsman from Tennessee, whose exploits in the Argonne Forest four months later were to make him a national hero. York's powerful religious convictions churned his conscience: he was prepared to serve his country, but could not bring himself to accept the need to kill a fellow human, until one of his officers persuaded him otherwise by reading to him from the Book of Ezekiel.

York's doughty deeds on 18 October 1918 were reported by the officers of the 82nd Division to General Headquarters thus:

The part which Corporal York individually played in the attack (the capture of the Decauville Railroad) is difficult to estimate. Practically unassisted he captured 132 Germans (three of

machine guns, and killed no less than twenty-five of the enemy, later found by others on the scene of York's extraordinary exploit. The story has been carefully checked in every possible detail from headquarters of this division and is entirely substantiated. Although York's statement tends to underestimate the desperate odds which he overcame, it has been decided to forward to higher authorities the account given in his own name. The success of this assault had a far-reaching effect in relieving the enemy pressure against American forces in the heart of the Argonne Forest.

York's feat was not, strictly, that of a sniper: but it was sharpshooting, and gallantry, of the highest order, and should have served to emblazon on the minds of generals the virtues of marksmanship even in a pitched battle. But there seems to be something in the higher-ranking military mind that blinds it to the obvious when it comes to preparing for war – as the next major conflict was to show.

GLOBAL WAR AGAIN

World War II broke out less than 21 years after the end of 'the war to end wars', but in many armies the sniping skills learned from hard experience in the previous conflict had been allowed to fade away. There was official recognition of the sniper in training manuals, but little was done to encourage or develop sniper training or tactics. Once again the Germans were the exception, and so were the Nazi Wehrmacht's most formidable foe: the Red Army of the Soviet Union.

The Red Army, like others before and since, learned the hard way. Attempting to annex Karelia, part of Finland, in the winter of 1939, the Soviet Union sent 1.5 million troops into the tiny country.

Right: An unsuspecting German soldier falls to the rifle of a Russian sniper at Stalingrad. The city was a sniper's paradise for both sides, although much fighting was within the range of sub-machine guns and hand grenades.

About a million never came home, while the Finns lost only 25,000 to the invader. According to historian Doug Bowser, at the end of the Winter War one Soviet general quipped glumly: 'We gained 22,000 square miles of territory. Just enough to bury our dead.' Finland, faced by potentially overwhelming strength, prudently ceded victory, but the Soviets did not press their territorial claims further, or indeed ever again, nor did they attempt another invasion. Superior knowledge of the terrain and brilliant use of resources gave the Finns what was in

effect a victory in the field, and among their resources were their hunters.

Finland had a long tradition of shooting (and still makes some of the world's finest hunting and target rifles), both on the target range and in the field. Rifles rather than shotguns were used by semi-professional hunters to shoot eider duck, using the more accurate single-projectile weapon, and immense skill, in order to protect and preserve the birds' valuable feathers. These men took to hunting Russians with a will, finding that Soviet columns moving

slowly through the Karelian forest made easy pickings. Among them were the all-time record holders in the annals of sniping, Simo Häyhä and Suko Kolkka.

Both men used nothing more elaborate than a Mosin-Nagant Model 28, fitted with 'iron' not telescopic sights. Haeyhae, credited with 505 kills during the Winter War, was a member of the Finnish 34th Infantry Regiment, a farmer by trade, and the winner of a mass of trophies for his skills with a rifle. He survived the war and was still alive and well, aged 95, in Spring 1999. Kolkka, who shot over 400 Red Army soldiers in 105 days, often took his war to the rear of the Soviet lines, with massive psychological as well as sanguinary effect in these supposedly safe areas. Kolkka was also no slouch with the submachine gun: he is credited with an additional 200 kills with this weapon during the same period. In one epic duel, Kolkka killed the Soviet sniper sent to hunt him down at 550m (600 yards) with a single shot after a running fight of several days.

The Red Army licked its wounds, but it had learned its lesson. Military historian Adrian Gilbert notes that:

> During [World War II] the Soviet military authorities promoted sniping throughout the Red Army. Their definition of the sniper's role was broader than that of the West, including general sharpshooting as well as dedicated sniping. Yet the Soviet military authorities made sniping a fully integrated part of infantry tactics, whereas in the West interest in sniping blew hot and cold, according to wartime expediency. Soviet snipers usually worked in pairs, and were allowed considerable freedom of action. They operated at a low tactical level, assigned directly to companies and platoons. There were normally large numbers of snipers available to junior infantry commanders who were used to handling them in everyday tactical situations ...

The Red Army sniper was expected to show more initiative than his rank and file comrades. He was informed that while raw German troops were careless and regularly failed to utilise available cover, seasoned troops were exceptionally cautious and the most artful stratagems were required to draw them into the open. In one instance, a Red Army sniper went into action with grenades and a bottle of combustible liquid. He hid them in an exposed area near enemy lines, then covertly withdrew to another well-hidden position before setting fire to the explosives with a single shot. The resulting blast drew the fire of German machine guns and mortars. Their positions were carefully logged by the sniper, who then set about silencing them, using either his own efforts or by calling on artillery support.

PATRIOTIC CHORES: VIETNAM AND AFTER

In other Allied armies, the story of sniping in World War II was depressingly similar to that in World War I:

Below: The US Army acquired the M21 version of the M14 (an updated M1 Garand), as its main sniper rifle in the late 1950s. Capable of fully automatic fire, it saw more use as a sniper support weapon than in its intended role.

M40/M40A1/M40A3

The original M40 was developed for the US Marine Corps for use in Vietnam, where the limitations of the .30-'06 Winchester Model 70 had become apparent, along with a drop in quality of the simplified M70s produced after 1964. Like many sniper-grade rifles made for the commercial and police market, it was based on the Remington 700-40 topped by a 3-9x variable Reddfield AccuRange scope. It was upgraded to the M40A1 (whose specifications are given above) in the late 1970s. Currently under development is the M40A3. According to the USMC journal *The Sentry*, 'The M40A3 comes almost directly from suggestions from snipers. Many features on the weapon, such as where and what shape the grips come in were discussed with members of both the sniper schools and the Fleet Marine Force. One example of the changes to the weapon is that in the past, a sniper had to adjust to their weapon, meaning if they had short arms or a high stock weld they would have to find a way around the problem. The new M40A3 comes with a new stock that has an expandable buttplate and adjustable cheek pad.' If the M40A3 passes the USMC's tests, it should have replaced all M40A1s in service by 2005.

Country of origin	USA
Calibre	7.62 x 51mm (.3 x 2 inches) and 9.652mm (.380 Winchester)
Overall length	1.12m (44 inches)
Barrel length	60.9cm (24 inches)
Weight	14lb 8oz

- Fibreglass stock with epoxy filler
- 10x Unertl telescope
- Mauser-type turning-bolt operating system
- Integral five-round magazine

harassed by enemy fire, soldiers had to be found and trained to learn the fieldcraft, the observational skills, the marksmanship and the bottomless patience all over again. Dedicated men – brilliant shots, often hunters in peacetime, with a talent for getting themselves noticed and for imparting their knowledge – came forward to fill the gap. With a few exceptions, it was not until the Vietnam conflict that Western armies finally learned the value of snipers, made them part of their infantry doctrine, and created the establishments to train them, hone their skills, and maintain their presence as a permanent part of the order of battle.

The top-scoring snipers in Vietnam include the US Marine Charles B. Mawhinny (103 confirmed kills) and the US army sniper Adelbert F. Waldron (113 confirmed kills); but the most renowned remains Gunnery Sergeant Carlos Hathcock, USMC, with 93 confirmed kills (and many more unconfirmed). If any one individual can be credited with fuelling this shift in the way the military establishment viewed snipers, it is probably Hathcock. The lessons he and others learned and passed on in the Vietnam conflict were used to make sniping a permanent fixture within the US military. After his retirement, Hathcock also pioneered sniper training and tactics among American police forces.

The rifle used by the USMC snipers was the Marine Corps-designed M40 fitted with 10 x magnification scopes. This rifle and its subsequent variations has served since the mid-1960s. Current

Above: A Marine sniper takes aim with his M40A1 from deep in the jungle of the Que Son mountains, March 1969. The tattoo is worn with pride, but would single him out for summary justice if he were to be captured by the enemy.

plans to update this weapon further for service in the first decades of the twenty-first century show its basic soundness.

Among his legendary achievements was the pinning-down and methodical destruction of a North Vietnamese army (NVA) company in the so-called Elephant Valley. After five days, Hathcock and his observer Corporal John Burke called down an artillery barrage to finish off the survivors, and withdrew. Hathcock's fieldcraft was unmatched: perhaps his greatest demonstration of his skills was a three-day stalk of an NVA general. Hathcock explained how he tracked down his quarry thus:

It was right at the end of my first tour in Vietnam, but I took the mission on myself because I figured I was maybe a little bit better than the rest of them. I was the one who trained them and I was supposed to be better. The stalk was about 1200 yards [1090m]. It took me three days and nights – and the morning of the fourth day was when I completed the mission.

I came out of the tree-line into open land, and I went onto my side. To go flat on my belly would have made a bigger slug trail, so I went on my side. Patrols were within arms reach of me; I could have tripped the majority of them, but they didn't even know I was there. I was in their back yard and they didn't suspect a one-man attack. And I knew from the first time when they came walder-gagging by me, that I had it made. This would be real good. So I just continued worming along.

There were two twin .51s [machine guns] on my left, two twin .51s on my right. And I could see the NVA cooking their groceries, and I was wishing I was there to have a little bit of it – I was that hungry and thirsty. But you got a job to do, you couldn't let any of that enter into it – it was just you and your bubble.

I crawled over a little rise, with my escape route out to the tree-line. I was in between all the .51s, which were set up for air attack, and I don't believe they could have got down that far [to engage me] – thank goodness! I saw all the guys running around that morning, and I dumped the bad guy at 700 yards [635m] – the distance I had zeroed my rifle in and the distance on the map. I estimated the wind, the temperature, the humidity, the whole ball of wax – trying to run it through my mind real quick. And it worked out right fair.

Then I had to get away. When I made the shot, everybody ran the opposite direction, because that's where the trees were. And it flashed through my mind, 'Hey, you might have something here.' So I went for that ditch, that little gully, and made it to the tree-line. I about passed out when I stood up, but standing gave me a little bit better speed. I had to look out for booby traps and everything when going back to my pick-up point.

Journalist Jim Spencer, in a .*Chicago Tribune* piece, revealed the following small, excruciating details of this exploit that Hathcock had modestly omitted from his account:

Hundreds of ants that had crawled inside his uniform dined greedily on his sweaty flesh. Forced to relieve himself in his pants, he stank of urine. He didn't need to worry about that problem any more. All he had to eat and drink the past 72 hours were a few cupfuls of water, parcelled from his canteen. His mouth was dry. Blisters covered his arm, hip and knee, where he had rubbed them along the ground.

Below: All modern armies include snipers equipped with a variety of sophisticated and specialised weapons. This Marine, from the Fleet Antiterrorism Support Team, was seen with his camouflaged rifle and scope on an exercise called 'Valiant Thunder'.

Military sniping today, in the major Western armed forces at least, is built on the experience of wars, like Vietnam, in the world's backyards. This is not simply because these armies have engaged in few campaigns that called for set-piece battles: the Vietnamese conflict was the archetype of the kind of brushfire wars that the major powers have had (or have chosen) to fight, and the enemies they have faced have typically been elusive guerrillas. Sniping, along with other guerrilla-like tactics short of terrorism, have proven one of the most effective means of dealing with such opponents. With dozens of such conflicts rumbling on in the last quarter of the twentieth century, the value of the sniper has had to be recognised by military planners and trainers.

All the major powers now maintain sniping schools, and there has been a constant exchange of experience and training techniques among them,

Above: Today's sniper has a role even in peacekeeping, where his long-range observation skills can often give the first warning of trouble. This Italian paratrooper in Bosnia wields an H&K MSG90.

notably between the US Marines and Britain's Royal Marines and Special Air Service. Ghillie suits have come far since the 95th Rifles adopted black and green as their uniform, and even since Lovat's Scouts introduced the ghillie suit proper into the British army. The weaponry has developed in interesting ways: the basic sniper's rifle is essentially the same as that used at the end of the nineteenth century, but the .50BMG round looks set to have a useful future.

The skills, and the extraordinary demands on the men who have them, remain essentially unchanged. So does the sniper's effect on the enemy. How devastating that can be, and what it takes to be a sniper, we look at next.

Snipers' roll of honour

Name	Conflict	Service Branch	Confirmed Kills
Simo Häyhä	Winter War	Finland	500+
Vasili Zaitsev	WW II	Red Army	400
Matthias Hetzenauer	WW II	Germany	345
Sepp Allerberger	WW II	Germany	257
Billy Sing	WW I	AIF	150
Adelbert Waldron III	Vietnam	US Army	109
Charles B. Mawhinney	Vietnam	RVN	103
Neville Methven	WW I	South Africa	100+
Carlos Hathcock	Vietnam	USMC	93
Dennis Reed	Vietnam	173d Airborne	68
Helmut Wirnsberger	WW II	Germany	64
Joseph T. Ward	Vietnam	USMC	63
Philip G. Moran	Vietnam	5th SFG(A) MACV-SOG	53
K. Tatang	North Sumatra	East Timor & Indonesia Armed Forces	41
Tom Ferran	Vietnam	USMC	41
William Lucas	Vietnam	US Army	38
P. Riel	WW I	Canada	30
J. Macormack	Ulster & Gulf	British Army	19
Gary J. Brown	Vietnam	US Navy	17
B. King	Ulster & Gulf	British Army	13
Joseph McElheny	Desert Storm	USMC	13

CHAPTER 2

THE MIND OF THE SNIPER

The psychology of sniping

'The mind is the sniper's greatest weapon'
—John C. Simpson

Above all else, the sniper is a hunter. The word 'sniper' comes down to us from game-bird hunting, while ghillies of the Scottish Highlands, who trained soldiers in the art of stalking, gave their name to the sniper's elaborate camouflage suit.

But the sniper differs from the game hunter in crucial ways. He is not generally engaging in a one-to-one duel of wits and skill against a naturally elusive and nervous animal. As well as a physical effect on his quarry, his activity has a psychological effect, and it is out of all proportion to his fire-power and his numbers. A sniper can hold up an entire army by stalling even a company-sized force, or by shooting a general. Unlike a deer or a lion, that enemy force will shoot back and otherwise do its utmost to eliminate the sniper – and will show him little mercy if he's caught alive. And he is not hunting for the pot or for the thrill of the chase but with the intention of killing a fellow, individual human being, one whose grin or grimace, or the twinkle in his eye, he can see through his telescopic sight.

Left: Above all, a sniper must be a man of patience, able to endure hours of discomfort before taking one perfectly judged shot. As important as his marksmanship is his skill at concealment, for a sniper who is detected has a very short career.

The man he has decided, calmly and methodically, to kill, may be indulging in the most intimate and innocent acts. Snipers have shot dead men who were swimming, having a bath, emptying their bowels, or enjoying a drink. None of the victims had any inkling that he was in the sights of his enemy and about to die.

Anyone with the ambition to be a sniper has to come to terms with this critical truth about his calling: he has to have what it takes to be a cold-blooded killer. An infantryman in the heat of combat is shooting at an enemy who may be little more than a blur, to try to preserve his own life as much as to defeat the opposition. On the rare occasions when he comes face to face with individual members of an opposing force in close-quarter or hand-to-hand fighting, he is supported by hours, even years, of indoctrination that the other man is somehow less than human.

At the critical moment, the sniper cannot fall back so easily on such simplicities. He may have been watching his target for days, learning his habits, getting to know his quirks – and always seeing him as a fellow human through the revealing eye of the telescope. A sniper has to be able to slaughter a human being whose unique qualities he may have observed for hours or even days, and who often presents no immediate, direct physical threat to him personally. In military historian Adrian Gilbert's words, the sniper is 'the ultimate hunter in a game where the quarry shoots back' – or, as World War II sniper Captain Clifford Shore put it, 'sniping is big game hunting *par excellence* – more skilful, more cunning, more serious and more dangerous since the "game" has an equal retaliatory power.'

A SENSE OF DISPROPORTION

The psychology of sniping falls into three essential parts: the effect of the sniper's work on the enemy; its effect on his colleagues; and the mental and emotional outlook and reactions of a potential or successful sniper.

Relentlessly accurate fire from a single hidden marksman can have a devastating effect on the morale of a sizeable body of troops. This has been acknowledged since the American War of Independence (1775–83), when the Kentucky rifles of the rebel colonists, firing as individuals, consistently outshot the volley fire from the smooth-bored muskets of the British redcoats.

One British veteran of the war, Colonel George Hanger, remarked that the colonials, who displayed 'unerring and surprising skill', were 'better marksmen than our regulars', because 'the American backwoodsman ... from the age of sixteen, has made the use, perfection, and construction of the rifle, and all other species of arms, both his study and his pleasure.' In addition, the difference in accuracy between the Kentucky rifle and the British musket Brown Bess was phenomenal. Hanger opined that with the Kentucky rifle an expert shot could place a bullet in the head of a man at 200 yards (180m). And if 'an American rifleman were to get a perfect aim at 300 yards [275m] at me, standing still, he most undoubtedly would hit me, unless it was a very windy day.' In contrast, Hanger considered that even a top-quality musket in good hands might hit a man at 80 yards (73m), and 'as to firing at a man at 200 yards, with a common musket, you may as well just fire at the moon.'

The sharpshooter's superior weaponry and his skill in using it brought a disproportionate sense of vulnerability to the enemy, then as now. In 1808 Captain Henry Beaufoy, in his charmingly titled *Scloppetaria, or Consideration on the Nature and Use of Rifled Barrelled Guns*, noted:

It has been readily confessed to the writer by old soldiers, that when they understood they were opposed by riflemen, they felt a degree of terror never inspired by general action, from the idea

Right: 'The Scout Davidson', a typical rebel sharpshooter of the American Civil War, with his Kentucky (more correctly Tennessee) rifle.

that a rifleman always singled out an individual, who was almost certain of being killed or wounded; and this individual every man with ordinary self-love expected to be himself. Destroy the mind, and bodily strength will avail but little in that courage required in the field of battle.

Faced by a general attack, even at squad, section, or troop level, a soldier can take some comfort from knowing that the enemy is almost certainly as frightened as he is, and equally unlikely to take level-headed, well-aimed shots, least of all at him personally. In the 1750s Major-General James Wolfe had (according to legend) trained his troops to

Dreyse Needlefire Rifle

- Small blade foresight, standing leaf rear sight
- Short range, probably not more than about 200m (220 yards)
- Turning bolt locked down with bolt to right

Country of origin	Prussia
Calibre	13.6mm (.535 inches)
Overall length	1.1m (43 1/4 inches)
Barrel length	69.8cm (27 1/2 inches)
Weight	4.5kg (10lb)

- One-piece stock and fore-end, secured to barrel by two bands and a nose cap

Developed in Prussia in the 1840s, this rifle was standard in Prussia from about 1841 and was adopted by other German states in the 1860s. The complication of this single-shot weapon's action was that the very long firing pin actually penetrated the cartridge to strike the primer seated at the base of the bullet. The pin was thus inside the cartridge case during detonation and suffered the consequential extremes of heat and corrosion. Nevertheless, the rifle served well enough until replaced after Prussia's war with France in 1870.

Russian Berdan Rifle M1868

Country of origin	Russia
Calibre	10.75mm (.42 inches)

- Turning-bolt action

The Russians fought the British in the Crimean War (1854–57) with smooth-bored percussion muskets. These were ancient then, having been converted to percussion from flintlock. The single-shot bolt-action Berdan rifle they adopted in 1868 is distinguished by a short, stubby bolt, which for reasons best known to people now

long dead was also a feature of their subsequent bolt-action designs up to and including the 1891/30 Mosin Nagant repeating rifle.

The Berdan's action was a development of the Dreyse needle-fire rifle, updated to take an American cartridge. Their cartridge was 10.75mm (.42 inches) and their 24g (370-grain) lead ball developed about 440m (1440 ft) a second, which is as fast as lead can go before it deforms – a problem that can be cured only by jacketing the lead bullet in copper or bronze.

This weapon served the Russians well enough until the rapid development of repeating-action rifles throughout Europe persuaded them, 20 years later, to buy a new design.

to wait until they could 'see the whites of the enemy's eyes' before opening fire – as well one might have to, if the notoriously inaccurate Brown Bess were to take any toll – and with such cool tactics won the Battle of Quebec against the French in 1759. But musket fire was as general in its intent as today defensive or 'suppressive' fire with fully automatic assault rifles is. One study found that for every musket ball that found a lethal mark, 460 were fired. In the Vietnam War, the first large-scale conflict in which both sides' infantry were routinely armed with automatic weapons, the received wisdom is that American footsoldiers fired some 20,000 rounds for every kill, whereas American snipers in Vietnam killed 10 men for every 13 rounds they fired. In a firefight, then, the average infantryman knows he has a pretty good chance of survival, even when being raked by automatic weapons. Being in the crosshairs of an unseen enemy who never seems to miss – or the constant fear of being there – is an entirely different matter.

The dread and consequent demoralisation that a sniper can instil, even in seasoned troops, may not be entirely rational, but such fear is comprehensible enough. A sniper may not down a great proportion of a unit's men, but he will (if he can) take out officers, gun crews, even support weapons and vehicles. If he kills an officer of field rank or above, especially one who is popular and effective, the practical blow of losing a key leader is naturally multiplied by a blow to general morale. If the sniper is also taking opportunistic shots at any soldier careless enough to expose himself, the perception of vulnerability to unexpected death grows and spreads throughout a unit.

After World War II, Clifford Shore questioned the men who had been under his command about the effects of being under various kinds of fire. He found that

the general opinion of the 'nerve shattering sequence' was that mental-unease under the varying types of lethal fire came in the following

Above: Russian soldiers, suitably attired in standard-issue, snow-camouflage suits, pick their way through the rubble of Stalingrad – the perfect environment in which both German and Russian snipers could hunt for their prey.

order – greatest effect first: sniping or aimed rifle fire; mortar fire; shelling; bombing; machine gun fire. In a way this was surprising, I had always felt that the men detested machine gun fire, and knowing their own very meagre gifts with a rifle I thought that they would have little respect for the Teuton riflemen, but no doubt this is just another example of the undue tributes paid to one's enemy.

A sense of being perpetually at risk, with no possibility of being warned of impending doom, and little or no chance of being able to fight back against an exasperatingly invisible enemy, can freeze a unit in its tracks. That – especially if allied to the common, if mistaken, perception that the enemy can shoot better than one's own side – in turn generates more fear, tension and frustration. Shore's modest survey was a modern echo of a note made in the *Order Book of the 5th Battalion, 60th Regiment of Foot*, early in the nineteenth century:

> The true rifleman will never fire without being sure of his shot. And he will recollect that a few well-directed shots, that tell, will occasion greater confusion than thousands fired at random and without effect, which only make the enemy despise our fire, and inspire him with a confidence in proportion as he finds us deficient in skill and enterprise.

Shore also noted how, in 1943 in Sicily, an entire battalion of the 51st Highland Division was pinned down outside the small village of Francofonte by the sniping of a few German paratroopers. Despite heavy shelling, the snipers, who were on usefully high ground, 'made some really remarkable shooting at ranges of 600 yards [548m] ... When they were eventually driven out by the advancing troops, the majority ... got away by the use of the most excellent fieldcraft.'

Eighty years before, in 1861, during the American Civil War, the *New York Post* reported that Hiram Berdan was recruiting crack shots for the Union Army's Corps of Sharpshooters. 'Posted in small squads at from one-eighth to three-eighths of a mile in the field, firing a shot a minute, and hitting their mark with almost dead certainty, they will be a great annoyance to the enemy. They will confine their attention to the officers and by picking these off, will bring confusion to the enemy's line.' This is exactly what Berdan's men went on to achieve on the battlefield.

Right: The hatred the sniper evokes amongst regular troops can be seen on the face of Private Thomas J. Barnes of the 503rd Infantry on Corregidor in the Philippines. A Japanese sniper's bullet missed his skull by a literal hair's breadth, February 1945.

L1A1 Self-Loading Rifle (FN FAL)

Country of origin	Belgium
Calibre	7.62mm (.3 inches)
Overall length	1.055m (41.5 inches)
Barrel length	.535m (21 inches)
Weight	4.3kg (9lb 9oz)

Following the war, Berdan devoted his energies not only to rifle design itself but also to that of the cartridges they fired. The Berdan rifle and cartridge of 1868 were the first to have the primer anvil fitted as part of the cartridge case, a design still used world-wide today.

Just over a century later, another distinguished sharpshooter, US Marine Thomas D. Ferran (a Vietnam veteran) commented thus on the psychological effectiveness of snipers: 'The idea of having your head blown off before you even hear the report of a rifle shot will demoralize a military unit quicker than an artillery round coming in. They can react to artillery because they can hear it, but not to a sniper's bullet.'

THE ONE AND THE MANY

Even a force that's knowledgeable about sniping and experienced in the field can be foiled by well-placed snipers. During the campaign to liberate the Falkland Islands in 1982, the British faced a numerically superior force of Argentinians, most of whom

Left: A Royal Marine escorts Argentine prisoners near Port Stanley at the end of the Falklands War. During the climactic night battles around Stanley, night-sight equipped rifles such as the FN FAL became de facto sniper rifles.

were holding open terrain broken by ridges, hills and rocky outcrops that made ideal defensive positions and provided perfect conditions for snipers. Among the Argentinians were some highly skilled marksmen. The British reduced the risks to themselves as far as possible by planning all their major engagements as night battles. The effectiveness of the snipers on both sides was reduced to those who were equipped with night sights. But not always – as Adrian Gilbert reports:

The one major exception was the battle of Goose Green, fought by the 2nd Battalion, the Parachute Regiment, against a large Argentinian force holding well-entrenched positions. Although intended as a night attack, the scale of the action ensured that the fighting went on into the next day. The snipers on each side were then able to engage in daylight shooting: the battleground was open and flat and bound on two sides by water.

As the British paratroopers were forced to break cover to advance along the Darwin Isthmus towards Goose Green, they presented relatively easy targets to the Argentinian snipers. A British source noted the accuracy of the Argentinian fire, explaining how a paratrooper 'went back under fire to retrieve a belt containing 100 rounds'.

Suddenly, he cried out and fell. He had been shot through the neck by a sniper's bullet, which broke his neck ... he was dead by the time he reached the ground.

Time and again British snipers had to be called in to eradicate the interference being run by Argentinian snipers. As the British campaign gathered momentum, that often became a luxury on the fast-changing battlefield, and Carl Gustav and Milan anti-tank weapons were used to blast the specially constructed sangars in which enemy snipers habitually holed up. Even so, as Gilbert

---

TCI M89-SR

Country of origin	Israel
Calibre	7.62 x 51mm (.3 x 2 inches)
Overall length	85cm (33 1/2 inches)
Length with sound suppressor	1.03m (40 5/8 inches)
Barrel length	56cm (22 inches)
Weight	4.5kg (9lb 1oz)

- Composite bullpup stock
- Any telescopic sight system
- Gas-operated, semi-automatic (M-14 action)
- Detachable 5-, 10- or 20-round box magazine

The M89-SR is designed as a dual-purpose weapon, for urban anti-terrorist operations as well as for battlefield sniping. The rifle is based on the M-14 in a bullpup configuration. The factory guarantees 1 MOA (examples tested have actually shot into 12.7mm (1/2-inch) bull at 92m (100 yards), or 1/2 MOA, which is unusually accurate for a semi-automatic action) and offers a full range of accessories and sales service. The rifle is compact, and is a kilogram (2lb 4oz) lighter than the US Army M24. The weapon is also known as the Sirkis M36 SR.

---

explains, the original manner in which the defenders deployed their marksmen gave the Argentinian riflemen considerable added value:

After the British victory at Goose Green the focus of action moved to the Argentinian troops holding Port Stanley [the capital of the Falkland Islands]. The Argentinians had prepared defences on the mountain tops surrounding the capital; apart from extensive minefields they had erected stone-built emplacements for their machine-guns and snipers. Argentinian snipers were despatched to stiffen the forward defences which, with a few exceptions, were manned by poorly trained conscripts.

Argentinian troops were well equipped with night sights, mainly second-generation models ... which were superior to the first-generation Starlight scopes used by the British. The infantry on both sides were armed with FN FAL [assault rifles], and the soldiers equipped with night sights on their FNs became the snipers during the final actions that decided the war. The British were impressed with the determination of the Argentinian snipers, who caused many casualties. During the attack on Mount Longdon, an entire British company was held up for hours by a single sniper. 'Men found themselves being hit more than once by the same sniper,' wrote one British officer, 'a terrifying tribute to the accuracy of the Argentinian's fire.'

That same year, the Israeli Defence Force (IDF) invaded southern Lebanon in an attempt to subdue the Palestine Liberation Organization (PLO) and its allies, who were based there. With the invasion force was Chuck Kramer, who had trained many Israeli snipers. He recounted later: 'I found to my surprise the PLO had very poor snipers, using equipment almost six or seven years old in comparison with modern Soviet equipment. [The USSR was the ultimate source for the majority of the PLO's arms.] They [the PLO snipers] worked alone with no sort of

Above: Urban environments such as Belfast provide endless sniping positions for insurgents, which in operations short of war cannot be cleared by traditional military methods.

training. They just went out to shoot as many Israeli soldiers as they could.'

One PLO habit was to spray a full magazine's worth of ammunition from an AK-47 assault rifle set to full-auto fire, in the general direction of the opposition, at utterly impractical ranges. Despite such conspicuous incompetence, the PLO snipers had a powerful effect on the invading Israeli infantry, who

were trained to support fast-moving armour. Said Kramer:

I found out – even as bad as [the PLO] were [at sniping] – the reaction of the Israeli soldier to being fired on by a sniper was terror. It was terrifying to feel you were under a sniper's scope. Units were stalled for hours while the commander was screaming for air support to take out a guy firing a plain Kalatch [AK-47 assault rifle] with no scope at 150 metres [165 yards] right into his position.

Barrett M82A1

Country of origin	USA
Calibre	12.7 x 99mm (.5 x 3.9 inches) (.50BMG)
Overall length	1.45m (57 inches)
Barrel length	73.7cm (29 inches)
Weight	12.9kg (28lb 8oz)

• Stock with stamped metal upper and lower receiver
• 10x Unertl (USMC M82A1A) sights, 10x Swarovski (commercial)
• Short-recoil, semi-automatic operating system
• Detachable 10-round box magazine

The M82A1 operates by means of the short-recoil principle. The 73.7cm (29-inch) Krieger barrel is fluted to increase rigidity and accelerate cooling. A twin-chamber 'chevron' muzzle brake tops off the barrel. This brake actively redirects the propellant gases rearward and has an efficiency rating of approximately 69 per cent, so that felt recoil is equivalent to no more than that of a 12-gauge shotgun. A Sorbothane recoil pad and rear grip help to maintain a firm, comfortable shooting position. The telescopic-sight reticle is calibrated to the ballistics of .50 BMG ammunition and provides range data from 500 to 1800m (550–1975 yards) and references for wind-induced drift. The M82A1 can be assembled in 30 seconds and field-stripped in 15 seconds. The weapon system consists of the rifle, two 10-round magazines, bipod legs, carrying handle and iron sights. Optional telescopes are available. A custom-fit airtight and watertight carrying case is standard equipment.

Though used as a sniper rifle, the M82A1 was first procured in 1991 during Operation Desert Storm, primarily for the US army Explosive Ordnance Disposal (EOD) units to disrupt unexploded ordnance. In EOD units, the Barrett M82A1 will be replaced during 2002 by a modified Barrett M95 bolt-action rifle. The Model 95 is a bullpup. It is 1.14m (45 inches) long, weighs 10.2kg (22lb 8oz) and has a five-shot detachable box magazine. It uses the same chevron muzzle brake as the M82A1. The recoil is similar to that of a .300 Winchester Magnum. The barrel, bolthead, bipod and pistol grip are all components from the M82A1. Like the M82A1, the Model 95 has an upper and lower receiver, which are linked together by two crosspins. By separating the receivers, the rifle may be disassembled. The rifle typically obtains 1 MOA accuracy.

Israeli snipers themselves are generally much better equipped than the oposition, and are issued with the TCI M89-SR, a version of the venerable US M14 developed in Israel and also known as the Sirkis M36.

British troops in Northern Ireland were also subjected to sniper fire whose wide-ranging psycho-

Left: Variations on this sign, with additions such as 'on hold' and 'I'll be back', have appeared around Northern Ireland during the Troubles. Most feared by the security forces were the two Barrett 'Light Fifty' rifles known to be in the hands of the IRA.

logical effects far outweighed its real tactical value. In August 1992, after a long lull in direct attacks on the security forces, the IRA began a sniping campaign that opened with the death of a British soldier standing in the market square in the border town of Crossmaglen, County Armagh. The following November an IRA sniper killed a Royal Ulster Constabulary (RUC) officer in County Fermanagh with a shot that could only have come from over the border in the Republic of Ireland. In 1993 skilled rifle fire killed several more members of the RUC and the British military. A member of the British Army commented ruefully – and with masterly understatement – that 'you don't get a kill on your first and only shot without a fair bit of practice ... We are facing a high degree of skill from these terrorists.'

The impact of the IRA's long-range shooting campaign was twofold. A rumour circulated that the lethal shots had been fired by a disaffected – or simply republican Irish – former member of US Special Forces. So, if the rumour were true, the average squaddie on patrol in Ulster had to face the possibility that he was at any moment liable to be pictured between the crosshairs of a gunman whose skills were very likely equal to those of any sniper in the world. Still more unnerving was the news that two or three of the effective rounds had come from a heavy-duty Barrett sniping rifle firing 0.5in Browning Machine Gun (BMG) rounds. Current military-specification 0.5in BMG ammunition includes a bullet that weighs 43g (665 grains), leaves the barrel at 885m/sec (2900 ft/sec) carrying an astonishing 16 kilowatts (12,000ft/lb) of potential energy. It is capable of destroying a house if fired in sufficient numbers, or disabling an armoured vehicle. The bullet retains enough energy to be lethal at well over a mile's range. The 'official' record for a kill with the BMG is held by US Marine Gunnery Sergeant Carl Hathcock who, while in Vietnam, felled a man with a scope-mounted M2 Browning machine gun with a single shot at a range variously estimated at between 2–2.3km (2200–2500 yards).

The IRA sniper and his kit made a fearsome psychological weapon system. This was indeed a psychological ploy, designed to affect British public opinion as much as the troops on the ground. Adrian Gilbert was told by a British sniping expert: 'What is interesting about the .5in IRA sniper is that the ranges were all within the effective capability of a much smaller calibre rifle, no shot being [made from] over 400 metres [440 yards]. The rifle was used for psychological and propaganda value.'

PAYING THE PRICE

Because of a sniper's disproportionately powerful effect on relatively large bodies of troops, one of the major drawbacks to answering the sniper's vocation is the ferocity of the reaction he can draw down upon himself. If detected or taken prisoner, a sniper can expect little or no mercy.

The least he can expect is a one-on-one duel with someone as skilled, experienced and cunning as himself. Then it's a case of the better man winning a contest of marksmanship, evasion and survival. Alternatively, and rather worse, the unit that he's been molesting will send out its entire sniping contingent to put an end to the nuisance, a move that greatly decreases his chances of escaping. At worst, he'll be thoroughly 'stonked' – his position demolished by artillery, tanks or mortars from the ground, or high explosive or napalm delivered from the air.

The classic instance of a one-on-one sniper duel took place at the siege of Stalingrad in 1942, between the Russian ace Sergeant Vasili Zaitsev and his German counterpart, Major Konings. Ziatsev's eventual victory was the fruit of immense reserves of experience, cunning, imagination, and almost infinite patience (see Chapter 5).

Heftier responses to aggravation from snipers contain an ambiguous lesson. Here is an illustration from New Guinea during World War II.

A battalion in the 163rd Infantry Regiment of the US Army's 41st Division took over a perimeter codenamed 'Musket' in January 1943. At once, they were assailed by a hail of fire from Japanese snipers in the surrounding jungle. Divisional historian Dr Hargis Westerfield recounts what happened:

Naturally, Jap sniper fire plunged down regularly at chow time. Once, we had the stoves set up and we had to leave the holes for food. Sniper fire

Right: The jungles of the Pacific provided as many hides for snipers as did the cities of Europe. This massive tangle of tree trunks on Guadalcanal held at least two until they were blasted out by artillery. The Marine at bottom left lends scale.

crackled in on us at any unexpected time in twenty-four hours. And at dusk, ground terrorists would probe into spots that snipers' binoculars had observed to be less protected. Lone men or small patrols would work around our flanks or rear, empty a clip or two rapid fire, then escape. Beneath the eyes of these killers, life quickly became not worth living unless we could shoot them out of the trees.

The Japanese, some of whom were shooting from ranges within the capability even of the most amateur rifleman, were clearly not always acting like snipers in Clifford Shore's severe definition of the term. And they were flying in the face of all current doctrine by hiding in trees. But they were deadly, both in terms of lives taken and morale depleted. The 163rd mounted a relentless response.

Our basic tactics consisted of three main steps – and a fourth which AT AT 163 [the regiment's anti-tank artillery troop] added with at least three 37s [37mm cannon].
    First we began to deal with Jap Perimeters Q-R which lurked in holes 20–30 yards [18–27m] before us. We set up two-man counter-sniper teams in slit trenches on the forward edge of the Musket perimeter. While one man quietly scanned the opaque jungle with field glasses ... the other man cuddled his well-cleaned rifle and waited. When the Jap shots rang out, the observer carefully spotted the green area where the shots came from. He pointed out the direction of the fire, let the rifleman observe through his glasses. Then the rifleman fired – until the Jap was silent – or Jap fire retaliated close enough to make him lie prone. Thus we secured our forward area.

Left: The sniper has often been best used as a defensive weapon, holding up enemy formations while his comrades regroup for a counter-attack. Seen duelling with a Japanese sniper is Marine private William Coffron, Solomon Islands 1943.

Garand M1C and M1D

- Blade foresight, rear peep; M1C sniper variant with Griffen & Howe or 2.5x M81 scope; M1D sniper variant with 2.5x M82 scope
- Gas-operated self-loading
- Eight-round magazine; rounds loaded in a clip ejected automatically with the last case

Country of origin	USA
Calibre	7.62mm (.3 inches)
Overall length	1.1m (43 1/2 inches)
Barrel length	60.9cm (24 inches)
Weight	4.3kg (9lb 8oz)

The Garand M1 (original version illustrated) was adopted by the USA in 1936 and some 5.5 million were made before production ceased in the 1950s. Two sniper variants were produced, designated the M1C and M1D. The clip-feeding system meant the telescopic sights had to be offset. A leather cheek piece was fitted to the stock to create a stock weld, and a short flash-hider covered the muzzle.

- Shoulder stock and lower handguard in one piece; separate upper handguard and fore-end secured by barrel band

Second, we sent counter-sniping teams into the trees on the flank and rear of Musket perimeter. To lessen the drudgery and danger of climbing among dead branches in jungle sweat, we set up homemade ladders. Usually we made them of telephone wire with stout wooden rungs.

Once the two-man tree teams were aloft, we got to work. We shot at all trees which seemed to harbor Nippo rifles. When Japs fired, we followed our standing order. All teams returned fire. If unsure of the actual target, we engaged probable Jap trees in the general direction of the popping fire. With our M-1s and 1903 rifles, we shot 200–400 yards [185–365m] ...

Third, we still needed another measure, because manning forward slit trenches with two-man counter-sniping teams was not enough. As soon as we posted sniper teams in trees, we could take the offensive. We could use these teams to guide attack patrols on the ground. We sent out small foot patrols of two-three men. Under direc-

tion from tree observers, our patrols shot down snipers or slashed other targets on the flanks of Jap Perimeters Q and R.

And the ground troops set booby traps – grenades tied to two separate trees and connected by a trip cord attached to the loosened firing pins. These booby traps caused Jap casualties, and once definitely effected our capture of a Jap Bren gun. Evidently the Jap had dropped the Bren gun when they fled from a grenade blast.

When we counter-sniped in these three steps, we carefully secured ourselves from accidentally shooting our 163 men. We briefed all our men on our methods. We located our own sniper trees so that nobody thought we were firing on him. Most important of all, we made it clear that nobody could fire on Jap snipers – except regularly designated counter-snipers.

Fourth, with the arrival of AT 163's 37mm cannon (at least three) we took another step against these hidden Jap killers ...

Methodically, AT's carefully aimed 37s [loaded with improvised grapeshot] were topping the jungle trees around Musket perimeter. For without tree cover, no snipers could operate. In BAR-man [Browning Automatic Rifle operator] Fallstick's opinion, the number of trees made the task hopeless, but he admitted that he saw a tremendous number of mangled trees on the horizon. Thus did 163 Inf's 1/Bn counter-snipe the

Nip snipers who took sight pictures on us from above Musket perimeter.

Adrian Gilbert's comment on this huge counter-

Below: Since the demise of the 19th-century Nock Volley Gun, counter-sniper weapons have tended to be whatever comes to hand. As seen here, a 37-mm anti-tank gun filled with grapeshot could prove effective against Japanese snipers hiding in the treetops.

Right: The German Army acquired a fearsome reputation for sniping in World War II, and among the most respected were those of SS units. This is a member of a Dutch SS battalion, taking aim across the wide Russian Steppes.

Above: An early attempt to extend the sniper's duties to the night hours was this infrared lamp and scope combination fitted to a Model T3 carbine used in Korea. The device was somewhat before its time but was the ancestor of several modern systems.

sniping operation is: 'If nothing else, the sheer size of the American operation was a backhanded compliment to the Japanese sniper.' But it was a little more than that. The 'compliment', after all, involved enormous effort, energy, expense, planning, and coordination of carefully trained troops, who might have been otherwise engaged in aggressive rather than defensive operations. The campaign took months to have any real effect.

Effective as snipers can be, they should be under no illusions about the kinds of reaction they may induce in others. Clifford Shore describes how, in 1944, one sniper attracted a devastating response to his depredations. Shore's unit was working between the rivers Maas and Roer, helping to drive the Germans out of Holland. During the advance, there was a hold-up 'at a little straggling village called St Joost':

The village commanded a wide stretch of the very flat countryside and it was essential that it should be taken. It was, however, very strongly held by some of those extremely redoubtable gentlemen, German paratroops, supported by tanks and SP guns [self-propelled artillery] ... The German paratroops were some of the bravest men our fellows had ever seen, or heard of, for time and again having been forced out of a position by the flame-throwers – not a pleasant business – they would come back before our men had established themselves.

Finally it was decided that one platoon of the company should be sent up to occupy the houses the others had won, leaving them to push on ... A visit by the company commander later in the day found the platoon in three of those Dutch houses with no hedges around them and completely open to view from ground-level up; the platoon was in great spirits but movement outside was distinctly tricky on anything but the home side ... because someone had been having cracks at his boys from another house about 400 yards [365m] away which was plainly visible and [the platoon sergeant] was convinced that he had singled out the window from which the shots were coming. Accordingly [the sergeant] produced his beloved [captured Mauser 86SR German sniping] rifle and settled down behind a chair in one of the windows to have a go at the first opportunity. Just as one of the officers was about to warn him that he might be silhouetted – as indeed he was – a shot came through the window, passed through the chair and missed the sergeant's head by a matter of a couple of inches. At that range it was a really good shot; a much shaken sergeant agreed. That shot marked the end of direct sniping activity there, for the common-sense, as opposed to

the sporting, way prevailed. A tank was called up, and the Jerry's house was very effectively sprayed by means of a couple of belts of Besa and the odd 75mm shell. Not sporting – not sniping – but effective, and War! There was no more trouble from that house.

Shore, an admirer of sniping talent regardless of where he found it, could not help wishing such a fine shot well, and added: 'Maybe that German sniper if he were as good as we thought had vanished before the tank proffered its visiting cards.'

A sniper who outstays his welcome for more than a second risks attracting massive retaliation. Anyone wishing to be a sniper has to build that thought into his picture of what his vocation entails, and has to be prepared for the possible consequences. This means he has to be ready to meet his fate in such a fashion, or feel confident that he can avoid it in good time. Sergeant Harry Furness, also a sniper in World War II, recounted that on one occasion

... I had good reason to think that my quick snap shot had hit a senior officer who was being shown our British front line area. He was with a group of others, and actually didn't present much of a target as they were behind some cover when I first spotted them some several hundreds of yards away. The officer who caught my attention was in the centre of the group using field glasses, when I chanced a very quick shot at him. Following my shot there was immediate commotion as they dropped behind cover, so I could not observe more.

I realised they would already be searching for my position with their binoculars, so I started to withdraw slowly backwards. But a furious retaliation barrage came down around my location very quickly indeed. It seemed to me they were firing everything they had, with machine guns, mortars and 88mm shell fire. The barrage they put down was continuous, with explosions and the screech of flying metal all around me.

Although I lay flattened out on the ground, several times I was lifted by the concussions. I had my mouth wide open with my arms wrapped around my face, for we had been told that more damage by explosions could occur if we had our mouth closed tight. I had been through many barrages previously but nothing on the scale of this never-ending retaliation, so I knew I had good reason to believe I had shot down a very senior officer. [S&K 107-8, account to AG]

EXPECT NO QUARTER

Understandably, snipers are not popular with their enemies. So powerful is the psychological effect of being a sniper's potential target that the written or unwritten rules of war tend to be suspended if a known sniper is taken prisoner. To judge from any number of war memoirs, snipers have routinely been shot out of hand, and without qualm, when caught alive. Qualified Wehrmacht snipers were awarded a distinctive badge from 1944, but few wore it, knowing what its display would bring if captured. As Harry Furness recalled, 'All snipers (on both sides), if captured, were shot on the spot without ceremony as [they] were hated by all fighting troops; they could accept the machine-gun fire, mortar and shell splinters flying around and even close-order combat, but hated the thought of a sniper taking deliberate aim to kill by singling them out.'

Perhaps less obviously, snipers are rarely regarded with unalloyed gratitude or admiration by those on their own side. A sniper may be respected, even held in awe, for his peculiar skills, but he can't expect to be popular. In part, perhaps, this is because most soldiers feel there is something faintly immoral or unfair about the sniper's one-way trade in death. The experience of the poet Robert Graves

Left: Looking more like extras from a Vietnam war film, a pair of Canadian snipers stalks a village on the road to Falaise, 12 August 1944. The specialist nature of the sniper's task has often allowed him more leeway in his dress than the regular infantryman.

during World War I, related in *Goodbye To All That*, gives the flavour of this ambivalent, even confused, attitude:

> Like everyone else, I had a carefully worked out formula for taking risks. In principle, we would all take any risk, even the certainty of death, to save life. To take life we would run, say, a one-in-five risk, particularly if there were some wider object than merely reducing the enemy's man-power; for instance, picking off a well-known sniper, or getting fire ascendancy in trenches where the lines came dangerously close. I only once refrained from shooting a German I saw, and that was at Cuinchy ... While sniping from a knoll in the support line, where we had a concealed loop-hole, I saw a German, perhaps seven hundred yards [640m] away, through my telescopic sights. He was taking a bath in the German third line. I disliked the idea of shooting a naked man, so I handed the rifle to the sergeant with me. 'Here, take this. You're a better shot than I am.' He got him; but I had not stayed to watch.

Such squeamishness would not have deterred Clifford Shore or any other dedicated sniper, but it was reflected among rank-and-file soldiers even as early as the American Civil War, as Adrian Gilbert notes: 'A Union infantryman recalled the unwritten code of honour that forbade soldiers firing on an enemy when "attending to the call of nature", but "these sharpshooting brutes were constantly violating that rule".'

In a striking image, Commando officer Derek Mills-Roberts recorded his own moral unease at seeing a sniper methodically go to work on a German gun crew during the Anglo-Canadian raid

Left: The church towers of northwest Europe were havens for snipers in 1944 until the advancing Allies blasted them with artillery as a matter of course. This tower at Hellimer in France was cleared by the British 6th Armoured Division in November 1944.

on Dieppe in August 1942, although his disdain for the target is clear enough: 'At last the rifle cracked. It was a bullseye and one of the Master Race took a toss into the gun pit. His comrades looked shocked and surprised – I could see it through my glasses. It seemed rather like shooting one of the members of a church congregation from the organ loft.' War correspondent Ernie Pyle expressed the instinctive feeling of his fellow Americans thus:

Sniping, as far as I know, is recognized as a legitimate means of warfare. Yet there is something sneaking about it that outrages the American sense of fairness ... [In Normandy in 1944, snipers] killed as many Americans as they could, and when their food and ammunition ran out they

Below: Ernie Pyle, 'The GI's friend' (centre), lived with and wrote about the average soldier, and knew well what they thought about 'sneaking' snipers. He is seen here with Marines on Okinawa.

surrendered. Our men felt that wasn't quite ethical. The average American soldier had little feeling about the average German soldier who fought an open fight and lost. But his feelings about the sneaking snipers can't very well be put into print.

However, on the static Western Front of World War I there was another, quite pragmatic, reason why British snipers such as William Carson-Catron (as they moved up and down the line of trenches) would be told, 'Push off now, do your stuff somewhere else'. B.A. Clarke was regularly offered 'cigs and tea so I would move on.' Sniper F.A.J. Taylor explains why, in *From the Bottom of the Barrel*:

Our lads in that front-line trench were never happy at our presence. They were quite naturally

Below: Recruits to the Lincolnshire Regiment hone their volley firing skills in the manner of wars past. The actual experience of the trenches that they would face would, however, see little call for this type of shooting.

P14 (Rifle No 3)

Country of origin	USA
Calibre (British)	7.69mm (.303 inches)
Calibre (American)	7.62mm (.30-'06)
Overall Length	1.17m (46.25 inches)
Barrel length	66cm (26 inches)
Weight	4.35kg (9lb 10oz)

• Integral five-round top-loaded magazine
• Subcontractors including Winchester; most manufactured between 1916 and 1918

• One-piece stock and fore-end separate over-barrel fore-end in wood; one barrel band and a nose cap
• Front blade sights, rear ladder to 1830m (2000 yards); long-range iron volley sights fitted to left side of stock; issue scopes on sniper versions including the 3x Pattern 1918 and 3x Aldis
• Turning-bolt action, Mauser pattern

This wasn't a Lee Enfield at all, although it was designed at the Royal Small Arms Factory at Enfield in England. It had a Mauser-type turning bolt, Mauser-type integral magazine and so forth, and was developed because the British National Rifle Association thought the SMLE not accurate enough. Had World War I not intervened, Britain might have adopted the P14, whose Mauser action made it far more accurate than the SMLE. Because of the war, the P14 design was made under contract for Britain by American gunmakers in .303 inches, and later as the M1917 for US forces in .30-'06. This is known to British civilian shooters as the P17, and to Americans as the 'Enfield rifle'.

P14 rifles saw limited service in World War II with Home Guard Units, where P17 variants chambered for the American cartridge were marked with red painted bands.

keen to maintain the status quo and thought we might stir up an enemy strafe and were apprehensive, venting their feelings by [hurling] the most blood-curdling curses in our direction. Their fears were not unfounded.

One day Taylor spotted a German sniper – who simultaneously spotted him, and sent a bullet that 'zipped viciously through the sandbags over my head'. An intelligence officer who borrowed Taylor's rifle and poked himself over the parapet to return the fire also enjoyed a near miss from the German's rifle, whereupon two Tommies nearby 'uttered loud obscenities and uncomplimentary remarks'. The officer scurried off to call down artillery on the sniper's position, which soon after 'went up in smoke'.

We watched ... a few surviving grey-clad figures hurry away and go to ground, and that was the last we saw of that enemy observer. My turn of duty over I moved away and as I passed the two lads in the adjoining bay, one said, 'It's all right for you buggers, but you go away and leave us to get all the shit.' And it came true as Jerry plastered that bit of trench in revenge.

OF HEROES SUNG AND UNSUNG

One might fairly surmise that most infantrymen find the sniper a difficult figure to contend with because he makes their stock-in-trade – death – all too uncomfortably clear. It is not easy to kill a fellow human, no matter how extreme the circumstances. Taking life is made less painful and onerous for the infantryman by training, indoctrination, and the impersonality and confusion of the average fire-fight. His weapons drop vague figures barely discerned at distances beyond any point of real recognition. There is an overriding desire to survive – to end the oncoming threat to one's own life.

Possibly most critical (and comforting) in the heat of a conventional infantry engagement is the knowledge that one is surrounded and supported by mates and buddies. It has become a keystone of modern infantry training in liberal Western democracies, where simple patriotism or regimental honour are often – albeit mistakenly – regarded as slightly outmoded, that when push comes to shove a soldier will fight on (and on) for the sake of those in his immediate unit, if for no other reason. And when one is side-by-side with them in the battle, it is often impossible to know exactly who may have killed which particular enemy. In this way, personal responsibility for breaking the commandment 'thou shalt not kill' is shared and diluted among a group of one's peers. The group as a whole can further, and usually fairly, plead in mitigation that, in any case, it was killing in self-defence.

In contrast, the sniper positively seeks to be a killer, and to kill in what most would regard as cold blood. But he is also prepared to take full responsibility for the deaths he causes. That takes unusually refined qualities of self-knowledge, independence, and resilience, quite apart from the extremely demanding specialised skills of marksmanship and fieldcraft involved. Killing people is, of course, part of the common footsoldier's job too. But the regular infantryman can blur or relieve the moral difficulties of killing in combat by appealing to the pressure of circumstances in a way that most people can understand. The sniper cannot fudge the issue in any of these ways. Nor would he want to, if the reflections of dedicated snipers on their work are any guide. Moral camouflage is the one kind of concealment that the sniper has to eschew.

The sniper is an outsider, regarded as a maverick even within his own profession, and that itself is one

easily, and often wilfully, misunderstood in societies that have enjoyed long periods of ostensible peace, with little or no direct threat to the population at large. The paradox, however, is that the sniper is the man who takes the logic of war to its ultimate conclusion: he seeks out the acknowledged enemy wherever he is, whatever he's doing, and calmly destroys him. He does this to cripple enemy plans, to save the lives of his comrades in arms, and in defence of his country or of the values it embraces.

By this reckoning the sniper ought to be widely regarded as a hero. Yet he is not. In failing to deny or obscure the fact that his trade is in death, he fails to acknowledge any great conformity with the herd, be it military or civil. This may seem

As a class, 'heroes' will often include those conventionally reckoned to be villains, if they are born in the mould of Robin Hood, Bonnie and Clyde, or the poet Lord Byron. Virtually every one diverges not just from the average, but from what is deemed to be the social norm.

If we examine our attitudes honestly, we maintain contradictory positions in our dealings with our heroes. We admire and honour them for their deeds or their art or their intellectual originality and courage, even for their humour – but in real life few really want to know them, and fewer still really want to be one, for the calling is too lonely or too dangerous (physically, emotionally, socially), and therefore too frightening. Heroes may be adulated by the mass of people, but paradoxically they are heroic because they are essentially outsiders.

To be a sniper means finding a place within the military or police, but that means living as an outsider in a subculture where conformity and convention are necessarily paramount, and which furthermore is one very long step removed from the peaceful easy self-direction of 'civilian' life. Thus the sniper is doubly isolated from the social conventions of both the broad and the narrow societies within which he lives. Royal Marine Mick Harrison positively embraced his solitude as a sniper:

Above: In today's wars, which are often civil wars and interethnic conflicts, the target is not always a military one. A city can be brought almost to a halt by well-placed snipers, as was Sarajevo in Bosnia in the early 1990s.

> I didn't bother with any back-up; it was just me against them. The sniper is the loneliest bloke in the world, and that's how I liked it. When I came back, the others could smell it on you, and they all wanted to get away. You didn't have any friends.

unduly harsh on the average soldier, who gets little enough thanks for his efforts anyway, but it's a fact of life that most people are made a trifle nervous by egregious characters – people who are just that little disconcerting bit more different or dedicated than the average. Such disquiet can only increase when that character's profession seems to stop just short of calculated homicide. Squaddies and grunts are not viewed, least of all in their own eyes, as paid hitmen.

Those who are half-feared, half-revered as nonconformists should at least be acknowledged as courageous, for it takes great inner resources to live on the fringes of a community, helping to sustain it even though by and large it does not care to accept you in any meaningful social sense. This is the sniper's uncomfortable position. To include sniping among the heroic vocations is not to glamorise the calling, but to recognise the immense strength of character that it requires, to acknowledge the subtlety and the directness of its moral position, and to see that the sniper is assuredly no weirder than other outsiders whom we find it easier to admire. The sniper is indeed a cold-blooded killer. And, strangely enough, that makes him peculiarly human. For, like it or not, history tells us that the ritual of war is central to human experience.

A HUNTER OF MEN

There is a school of thought, which only those who have seen combat have the right to debate, that warfare is one of the supreme human experiences. In 1935, Captain Herbert W. McBride made the classic statement of this position in his book *A Rifleman Went To War*. He was an American marksman, a combat-proven sniper and Indiana National Guard officer who joined the Canadian Army in 1914 so as 'not to miss the fun' (the USA entered the conflict only in 1917). He says: 'A man may know all the [military] text books by heart and be able to repeat them forward and backward, may be an expert rifleman and all that, but it is only in actual combat that he can find himself.'

If one regards the sniper as embodying the finest qualities of the modern infantryman – while, at the same time, bringing his own special expertise to bear on his work – then one will be inclined to see his vocation in its true light. The sniper is the foot-soldier who has, in a sense, already found himself. But this is not a calling for the fainthearted, nor is it one for the amateur. And to be effective, the sniper needs someone with the military imagination and opportunity to find him and make use of his idiosyncratic characteristics. That the sniper is a huge asset to an infantry unit has had to be re-learned by established armies in virtually every significant conflict since the virtues of marksmanship combined with cunning became evident in the American War of Independence. The price of repeated ignorance has been many lives vainly squandered; the dividend has been a small but

intensely enthusiastic literature rich in advice, derived from real experience, on the qualities of those who make the finest snipers.

Those who belong to that select band may be taken to have already mastered the most subtle points of camouflage, movement, marksmanship and observation. Even so, the consensus of opinion is that a man with the spirit of the hunter, and perhaps ideally the experience of the hunter, makes an excellent potential sniper.

Erich Kern, in *Dance of Death*, described meeting German snipers on the Eastern Front during World War II in these terms:

> We met more of them farther along the line, this time two boys from the Siebenbuergen, Rudolf aged 19 and Michael aged 24. We talked to them about their homes, about the war, about everything. Rudolf's father was a huntsman, his brother a huntsman, and he had it in his blood. Put a gun in his hand and his eye looked for a target. Michael had seen his first hunt while still a boy. Now they were back at the butts, but here the quarry fired back. 'We must only fire occasionally and we have to hit them when we do,' Rudolf said, his eyes alight, 'otherwise we give ourselves away.'
>
> A Red Army man showed himself in the opposite trench. A quick aim, then 'Crack!' and he fell forward. A hit? – or had he merely ducked for cover? More hours of waiting and then at last a target. Another shot. The man on the other side stopped and tilted over backwards. A pencil mark on the stockade – that one counted. I asked what they thought about as they stood there crossing them off one after another. 'Only that there's one more gone; one less to hold a rifle,' they said.

Yet what is perhaps most striking about this account is the matter-of-factness with which these young Germans transformed their skills at hunting game or reducing populations of animal vermin into killing humans. A man may be a brilliant hunter, but

to be a sniper he has to have an almost superhuman capacity to accept the irremediable finality of his effect on a human target.

As the US Army's 1989 training circular *Sniper Training And Employment* so impersonally puts it: 'the sniper must not be susceptible to emotions such as anxiety or remorse. Candidates whose motivation toward sniper training rests mainly in the desire for prestige may not be capable of the cold rationality that the sniper's job requires.' It would be nearer the truth to say that snipers, especially those who were

Above: The modern sniper isn't necessarily a professional soldier and not necessarily a man either. Naidia, aged 22, plied her trade from her apartment in Sarajevo during the Bosnian Civil War.

conscripted into the wars in which they found themselves, have had to discover a way of sidestepping anxiety or remorse if they were to survive the demands of their work.

A sniper's first real kill is the test of his ability to accept the peculiar nature of his task. Corporal (later

Above: A British Paratrooper trainee sniper practises with his Parker Hale M85 rifle. He will then learn the fieldcraft and stalking techniques that will help keep him alive.

Sergeant) Jeffrey Clifford, a US Marine scout sniper in Viet nam, reported his own first success as a sniper thus:

The Hill 55 area was mostly flat with a few rolling hills. I guess a first kill is always an unforgettable experience. I certainly will never forget mine. 'She' was about 18 and was carrying an M1 carbine. At the time I did not know that he was a 'she', and, of course, I did not know she was pregnant. The shot was overlooking a free-fire zone (which was a slightly elevated plateau) outside a deserted villa. A small VC [Viet Cong guerrilla] patrol broke from the treeline and was re-entering it when I took out 'tail-end Charlie'. The shot was about 600 yards, through the lower back and out the front. The body and rifle were recovered, the kill confirmed. The grunts gave me credit for a 'two with one shot'. I took solace in staring at the sun. [Sergeant Jeffrey L. Clifford, 'In His Own Words' in Chandler and Chandler, *Death From Afar*, Volume II (Iron Brigade Armory, Maryland) p44]

In World War I, Victor Ricketts was a sniper for the British Army, and found this way to deal with the stress of the job:

It's not too pleasant to have a fellow human being in one's sights with such clarity as to be almost able to see the colour of his eyes and to have the knowledge that in a matter of seconds, another life will meet an untimely death. However, one had to be callous; after all it was an eye for an eye, a tooth for a tooth.

The hunter's skills and the ability not to get caught at it (a vital talent for a sniper) were at the back of Clifford Shore's mind when he said: 'the general maxim to the sniper was that he should attain the standard of the highly skilled and cunning poacher.' The pioneer of British Army sniping in World War I, Major H. Hesketh-Prichard, would have agreed:

The truth of the matter forced itself upon me, as I spent day after day in the trenches. What was wanted, apart from organisation, was neither more or less that the hunter spirit. The hunter spends his life in trying to outwit some difficult quarry, and the step between war and hunting is but a small one.' [Major H. Hesketh-Prichard, *Sniping in France: With notes on the Scientific Training of Scouts, Observers and Snipers* (Hutchinson, n.d.) p13]

His contemporary Herbert McBride echoed these sentiments in these words:

Since we no longer have an open season on Indians, about the best way to acquire the skill to advance over varied ground without being detected is by stalking wild game. And by stalking, I mean to get right up close to the animal before taking the shot, and not merely to crawl into some position at long range from which it is possible to take a shot over open ground. Crawl, roll or push yourself forward until you are within relatively close range of the target, and learn just what sort of Indian-cunning and patience the art of stalking calls for. [H. W. McBride, *A Rifleman Went To War* (Small-Arms Technical Publishing, 1935), p300]

Unlike a human being, who can be distracted by all kinds of trivia from a task in hand, an animal is almost constantly on the alert for potential predators. In Europe, large game like deer and small vermin like foxes no longer have any so-called 'natural' predators. But millennia of avoiding attacks by bears and wolves have bred a population fully alert to the dangers represented by people. Hunting game and foxes successfully calls for considerable fieldcraft, but also a cool nerve for the moment when the quarry is finally in the sights.

HARDENING THE HEART

Not everyone, even those with years of game hunting behind them, can make the transformation from stalking animals to shooting men. For some, even the shift from target shooting (in which they may be expert) to killing live quarry can bring about a failure of nerve. Clifford Shore noted:

During the training of snipers there were many instances of men being excellent target shots but failing in the role of sniping shots. Psychologically, the difference between resting on a placid firing point and shooting in war, even if one is in a comparatively safe position oneself, is the greatest possible contrast. Even in hunting the difference is most marked and I have had

personal experience of good target shots failing lamentably in the hunting field with its nerve tensions resultant of growing excitement.

If the shift in psychological gear can be made, a massive emotional armour comes into play. US Marine Captain Stephen L. Walsh, a sometime chief instructor at the USMC sniper school, has said: 'We have the capability to watch people die; his head explode or whatever. It's the mark of a true professional to carry out the mission.' But being a 'true professional' is not always without its cost to the sniper's humanity, and the price can sometimes take the form of a radical failure of imagination. A sniper instructor with Britain's Parachute Regiment illustrates the point:

The average paratrooper tends to be a bit more aggressive or more rugged than normal. As an example of their black sense of humour, we went down to Hythe on the OP range [which recreates urban conditions in Northern Ireland]. There are moving targets on each street, and you start with very simple black and red targets of which the red has to be engaged. The idea is that it is progressive, so that you can eventually distinguish between targets and identify the one that appears carrying a gun. We had one pair of snipers in the roof overlooking a target of a woman and a pram. The woman was shot, and the company commander running the range said: 'Well, that's another orphan child to add to the problems of Northern Ireland.' At which point there was another shot, and it went straight through the pram.

The realistic prospect of the consequences of taking such a shot (even in error) calls for a different kind of fortitude than that required on the battle-field, but one that is no less crucial for a sniper to have – especially in an era in which most large-scale military deployments are 'peacekeeping' missions. In December 1992, US Marines led the way for just such an American presence in Somalia, hoping to separate the feuding warlords who had left the country without an effective government. A letter home from a US sniper instances some of the disinformation that the Somalis fed the press:

I'm sure you've read the wonderful story that is floating around the US from an [Associated Press] reporter here. The Somalis here are well known for fabricating stories for the Press after we engage. In one incident I was accused of killing 12 people with one bullet.

On our last engagement we took out a man on top of a truck armed with an RPG [rocket-propelled grenade]. The Somalis said we had killed a pregnant woman. An Army CID team was flown in from Washington the next day. A forensic expert examined the so-called victim and determined she had been hit by a moving vehicle and not by a .50-calibre bullet. By the time this was discovered the reporters had already written their stories that stated we were killing innocent women and children with hunting rifles and .50 calibre anti-armor weapons. [Letter written to Jim O'Hern, and reproduced in Chandler and Chandler, *Death From Afar*, Volume III (Iron Brigade Armory, Maryland), p.158]

PATIENCE IS A VIRTUE

When the US Army's 9th Infantry Division began its own sniper training programme in Vietnam in early 1968, the instructors looked for candidates who at least approached their ideal. He would be a good, conscientious soldier, a 'solid citizen' who was also a good team worker. He would also be a 'daring-type person', and one who remained cool even when under extreme pressure. When they are found side by side in one individual, these qualities clearly make up a character considerably more

Left: Intervention in Somalia in 1993 turned to disaster for the Americans. Mogadishu in particular was a (Somali) sniper's paradise, with a multitude of good firing positions and, sometimes, a compliant population to hide amongst.

complex than a simple gung-ho soldier, and their rarity may well explain why so few who want to be snipers succeed in surviving the rigorous courses of training.

If a sniper needs anything to accommodate the realities of his job, on – and perhaps particularly off – the battlefield, it is the quality of patience. Time and again experienced snipers and sniper trainers have emphasised the need for patience.

The legendary US Marine sniper Carlos Hathcock had no time, as an instructor, for hotheads, psychopaths or those lacking emotional discipline. During his second tour of Vietnam, one trainee proposed using some Vietnamese farmers for target practice. 'We let him go,' Hathcock recounted, 'put him back in the line company. He just wanted to

shoot somebody – anybody. Snipers aren't trained that way. You have to train your mind to control every emotion you have.' Hathcock was clear about what he wanted in a sniper, and his requirements were at least as complex as those of his colleagues in the US Army:

I like someone who is quiet, malleable, knowledgeable, able-borne, very highly intelligent, with a knowledge of fieldcraft and weapons, and an ability to observe and get their observations down in writing. You've got to have the utmost patience; I've lain three days in one spot, just observing. To be a good shooter you need a good head on your shoulders, and to be able to absorb everything that is going on around you.

M14/M21/Springfield M1A

- Gas-operated self-loading; selective single-shot or full automatic fire (M14); semi-automatic only (M21)
- Detachable 20-round box magazine

Country of origin	USA
Calibre	7.62 x 51mm (.3 x 2 inches)
Overall length	1.12m (44 1/8 inches)
Barrel length	55.9cm (22 inches)
Weight	3.9kg (8lb 9oz)

- One-piece wooden shoulder stock and fore-end; synthetic (or metal) top handguard; M21 sniper variant with a selected-walnut stock impregnated with epoxy resin and glass fibre bedded with the receiver to add stiffness
- Iron sights, usually a tunnel foresight and rear peep; various optical sights can be fitted to side mounted telescope fitting; issue M21 with variable 3-9x Redfield AccuRange scope

During the late 1950s the M14 replaced the M1 in US service. It was essentially an M1 rechambered for the new Nato standard 7.62 x 51mm round. Robust and well-made, the M14 was heavy, weighing in at 5.1kg (11lb 4oz) fully loaded. In its full automatic-fire mode, it was difficult to control. In semi-automatic variants the M21 has become useful to snipers, however, as a spotter's back-up weapon, capable of fast, accurate, defensive fire. This is a more practical application than the primary sniping role envisaged for the US army's M21. With an eye to the police market, Springfield Armory produces the M1A National Match, a version of the M21 with a heavy match-grade barrel, improved internal springs and trigger unit, adjustable cheek-piece and bipod. This has proved highly effective as an anti-vehicle weapon with a number of American police units.

You need a pure, absolute concentration on the job you are doing – I call it getting in my bubble. [Gunnery Sergeant Carlos N. Hathcock, from video recording *Carlos Hathcock: Marine Sniper* (LOTI Group in association with Paladin Press, 1994)]

Hathcock's fellow Marine sniper Mark Limpic too was aware of how infrequently the necessary traits were to be found, even among supposedly specially selected and fully trained snipers in Viet Nam. He insisted that patience was both a virtue and an extremely rare commodity among Americans:

I remember how hard it was to train – to instill – patience in new snipers, the patience to sit on

Above: In wartime, and particularly with a conscript army, as in Vietnam, the sniper instructor has to be wary of the 'self-selecting' candidate. Many soldiers see becoming a sniper as a way to stand out and to become a hero.

your butt for hours, waiting to get a good shot. Most new men get pretty excited upon seeing an enemy or two, and want to immediately get a shot off. One particular incident comes to mind.

I took a couple of scout snipers out from Hill 65 and set in by the river. After a few hours several NVA soldiers came out of the undergrowth to cool off in the river. My snipers wanted to crank some rounds into them – so much for patience.

I held them back, told them to sit tight, and to observe. I reasoned that more swimmers would probably come, and those who were already there would get deeper into the water – which is damned hard to run in. We waited, and they came. We got off a number of easy shots and some that were harder. We obviously screwed up their party. I cannot remember how many we killed, but there were more than a few. All due to our patience.

That was one of the times I feel I taught the young studs to do better. They learned that patience is essential. Most Americans can't sit

Below: A British Army sniper aims his Lee Enfield through a hole in an ancient Aden wall. Incredibly, this basically 19th-century rifle nearly made it into the 21st.

still for more than 10 minutes, and the self-discipline to do so requires convincing training. [Mark Limpic, 'Sniping: The Virtue of Patience' in Chandler and Chandler, *Death From Afar*, Volume IV (Iron Brigade Armory, Maryland)]

STAY COOL

Allied to the sniper's capacity for patience is (as the US Army recognised) his ability to stay cool no matter what is happening around him; and in this he especially resembles the dedicated and experienced game hunter.

Some snipers have emphasised the personal, individualistic nature of their way of fighting without seeming to recognise this. US Marine Craig Roberts seemed to follow his calling with vengeance in mind:

> Killing like this was personal, not like in a fire fight when it was difficult to tell who killed who. Through the scope you could see the expression on their faces in that instant before you sent a bullet screaming into their flesh. Mostly they were young faces, some no older than sixteen. I was just nineteen, so their youth had little impact. We were doing something personal to avenge Marines who had been killed and maimed by mines, booby traps, and snipers.
>
> Going to the enemy on his own turf and killing him was better than waiting until he came on yours. We were seeing the enemy – and he was ours.

Royal Marine Mick Harrison broke all the rules of fieldcraft in his enthusiasm to get kills during his tour in Aden in the 1960s:

> I had to make the terrorists show themselves. What I did was to expose myself to them deliberately. I'd kill one, then I'd move to a new position. They were about four to five hundred yards away. I'd get up and wave to them to draw their attention. It was the old idea of bringing

your quarry to you. They thought they were good and I let them come to me. The first person I shot came out all dressed in black, and I remember I shot him in the throat. They wanted to go to Allah's garden, and I just paved the way for them.

But the sniper who can't count on his enemy's incompetence at counter-sniping and wants to stay alive would do better to remain cool. Sniping is a personal war, but it calls for a mindset in which, in journalist Jeff Stein's words, 'a man has to put his soul on hold'. As Clifford Shore maintained:

> The average American and Englishman is averse to killing and many, having been forced to kill, suffer from remorse. But it is a fact that a sniper will kill with less conscience-pricking than a man in close combat. Personal feelings of remorse or questioning of motives will slow down a man's critical killing instinct and the sniper who allows himself to fall into such a train of thought will not last long. It is imperative to look upon the killing of an enemy as swatting a fly, an unthinking automatic action. Two things only should really interest the sniper – getting the job done and getting away unscathed.
>
> To become accustomed to 'sniper killing' is not so difficult or hard as close-quarter killing. A man dies more slowly than the average person thinks; he often grins foolishly when he's hit, the whites of his eyes roll upwards, death sweat gleams on his forehead and he sags to the ground with a retching gurgle in the throat – and it is difficult to hear that gurgle without emotion. The sniper is usually spared all this unless he's quick enough to get his binoculars on his victim, or the 'sniped' is at such close range that the telescope sight will give him all the motion pictures he needs.
>
> Sniping is not the vague, haphazard shooting of the unknown in a sort of detached combat. It is the personal individual killing of a man in cold

blood, and is an art which must be studied, practised and perfected. I often heard it said that a sniper should be a man filled with a deadly hatred of the Hun, or enemy. But I found that the men who had a seething hatred in their hearts for all things German, such as those who had lost their wives and children and homes in blitzed cities, were not the type to make good rifle killers. The type I wanted was the man of cold precision, the peace-time hunter who had no hatred for his quarry but just a great interest in the stalk and the kill.

For Shore, excitement came only with the kill:

When one was in position for a shot there came an 'inner freezing'; the breathing was not quite normal; the hearing sense was magnified and there came too that sense of excitement which all hunters know and which results in an unconscious nerve-hardening, and once the Hun was in the sight and the pointer steady at the killing spot there was no qualm of conscience about hitting him or taking life. The true hunter is never a butcher; he does not desire to kill for killing's sake, but there is something elemental in the stalk and the slaying which swamps every other feeling and makes the heart and brain exultant ...

WHAT IT TAKES

'It takes a special kind of courage to be alone; to be alone with your thoughts, to be alone with your fears, to be alone with your doubts. This courage is not the superficial brand stimulated by the flow of adrenaline. Neither is it the courage that comes from the fear that others may think one a coward,' wrote Charles Henderson in his biography of Carlos Hathcock. He continued:

Honor on the Battlefield is a sniper's ethic. He shows it by the standards and discipline with which he lives life in combat. By the decency he shows his comrades and by the rules he adheres to when meeting the enemy.

The sniper does not hate the enemy; he respects him or her as a quarry. Psychologically, the only motive that will sustain the sniper is the knowledge that he is the best person to do it. On the battlefield hate will destroy any man – and a sniper quicker than most.

Shore's and Henderson's accounts of the sniper's profile and his motives are doubtless accurate, but they are limited. The sniper needs the courage to work alone in often appalling conditions and to take human lives with a clear conscience. Of all the psychological traits of a successful sniper, the stamina to withstand moral solitude, on or off the battlefield, is probably the single most important. Analyst David Reed asks of anyone wanting to be a sniper:

Ask yourself this – Do you have a hot temper? Do you anger quickly? Anger causes the pulse to quicken ... and may cause careless or irrational behavior, all of which are bad. Do you like to hunt? Do you like to hunt alone? Have you ever spent an entire week alone? No television, no phone, no friends, no family, no nothing? Have you ever gone camping alone? In a remote area where you saw no one? How did it make you feel, what did you think about? What did you do while you were there? How many times did you masturbate? How often did you eat? Was there a difference in your mental state on the first day and the last? Snipers are not necessarily 'loners.' In fact, someone who has problems relating to other people may not make a good choice.

To maintain a moral coherence, Reed implies, requires a powerful connection with the social world, however far and distant that world may be. It is the knowledge of social values that sustains one when in solitude, cut off from the community.

Sniping often combines bodily as well as mentally horrible work, too. Internet journalist 'Condor', writing in his regular feature 'From The

THE MIND OF THE SNIPER

High Ground' for the Sniper Country website, noted in August 1996 the combination of psychological, emotional and physical stresses a sniper has to withstand:

Try to imagine the worst way of life you can. Now, multiply that times 14. Now square it. Now add 400. That being done, you're nowhere near what it's like to be in the military as an enlisted man, or as an officer ... oh, and did you say you

wanted to be a sniper? Oh, well, in that case, you can also add:

Little or no support in an operation you're on that goes bad, crapping in your pants and urinating in your pants because you can't run off to a

Below: Backed up by his trusty observer, Sfc B. Moore of Company B, 182nd Regiment, 2nd US Infantry Division takes aim on a target, Korea, 29 May 1951. Note the flash suppressor, and the characteristic offset scope of his M14 sniper rifle.

latrine because you'll blow your stalk or give away your hide, running out of food, equipment that was built by the lowest bidder (including your weapons and optics), failure to receive credit unless you've got a 'confirmed' kill, watching through your scope as the bullet you just launched takes off the head, from the nose up, your target – then living with what you've

done, and doing it again and again and again – bugs, bugs, bugs, and more bugs ... bugs you've got on you that you can't swat for tactical reasons, bugs that can kill you, bugs that you've got to eat because you've run out of food (did I mention little or no support while you're on a mission?), if you're caught you could be sliced, diced, tortured, raped (yes, raped), skinned alive and then killed 'just because' you're a sniper (snipers get 'special' treatment by the enemy) ...

Sniping isn't just killing people. It's B.S. [bullshit], too. You can't forget the B.S., because it's always there, no matter what rank or job you have. As a sniper, you're an intelligence gatherer, you make and file reports, you have to not engage targets that you 'know' you should (because your unreasonable-but-legal orders forbid it), and all the time ... someone is trying to hunt you down, to kill you, because you're a sniper! Fun? It's not fun, it's B.S., and it's just a job. Snipers support the mission, support the commander, and save lives. It's tough work and it's not glamorous.

But Condor's bluntest words are reserved for the sniper's real business – killing – and how difficult it is to deal with:

Killing people is 'grown up' business, it's not for kids. If you are a kid, you won't be after your first kill. Never again. No more innocence. You can't go back [...]

Think what you have to in order to do the job, but when it's over, really over, remember that the 'targets' you 'serviced' were once living people, and they aren't anymore because of you.

Left: The sniper's duties are as much that of the forward observer as the trained killer, which is why they are often attached to reconnaissance units.

Right: Though the sniper mainly works alone – but always as support for a larger team – and is prepared to kill a possibly unarmed opponent, he is not a psychopath or a hothead.

CHAPTER 3

THE APPRENTICE ASSASSIN

Sniper deployment and training

'Second place in this environment equals an end to everything'
—Sergeant Lance Bacon, USMC

In an attempt to persuade the Canadian Army that it needed to maintain and improve its sniper establishment and training, Major R. Bagnall gave a lengthy and useful definition of what snipers actually do, both on the battlefield and in urban warfare:

A sniper has special abilities, training and equipment. His task is to deliver discriminatory, highly accurate rifle fire against enemy targets which, because of range, size, location, fleeting nature or visibility, cannot be engaged successfully by the typical rifleman. By delivering precise long-range fire on selected targets, the sniper creates casualties among enemy troops, curbs enemy movement, terrorizes enemy soldiers, debases morale, and influences their decisions and actions. By augmenting a unit's firepower and enhancing the varied means for destruction and harassment of the enemy, the sniper propagates the combat power of that unit and hence becomes a 'combat multiplier'.

Left: A sniper and observer team from the Spanish airborne forces pathfinder group take part in a EUROFOR exercise in southern France with a night-sight equipped Barrett M82A1.

Parker Hale Model 82

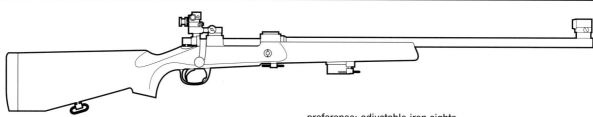

Country of origin:	United Kingdom
Calibre:	7.62 x 51mm (.308 Win)
Overall length:	1.16m (45.8 inches)
Barrel length:	65.7cm (25.9-inch), free floated heavy
Weight:	4.8kg (10.58lb) empty without scope

• Selected wood stock, extendable using butt spacers
• Sights: mounts for telescopic sight of customer's preference; adjustable iron sights
• Turning bolt operating system: based on the Mauser 98 action
• Four-round integral magazine

The Parker Hale M82 is the basis for the Canadian armed forces' C3 and the Australian Army's L3 sniper rifles. The makers maintain it can deliver precision fire at all ranges out to 400 metres with a 99 per cent chance of first-round accuracy. The V2S 4-9 variable power x 10-mm telescopic sight can be factory fitted. An optional, adjustable bipod is also available.

C3A1

Country of origin	Canada
Calibre	7.62 x 51mm (.308 Win)
Overall length	1.16m (45.8 inches)
Barrel length	65.7cm (25.9 inches)
Weight, without scope	4.8kg (10lb 9oz)

• Barrel heavy, hammer-forged, free-floating
• Wooden stock; target beavertail; with accessories rail; receiver epoxy-bedded
• 10x Unertl sights; iron sights for back up
• Turning-bolt operating system (modified Mauser 98)
• Integral four-round magazine

The C3A1 is the Canadian army's issue sniper system. Based on the Mauser 98 action, the original C3 (adopted in the 1970s) was a Parker-Hale Model 82 with Kahles Helios ZF69 6 x 42 telescopic sights, new rifling and a bolt handle modified for use with gloves. The more recent C3A1 uses the same Unertl 10x scope used in the USMC M40A1 rifle. The Model 82 is a favourite with competition shooters and has won many matches. It was also adopted by the Australian and New Zealand armies, and in the British army is used as a target rifle for cadets.

Doctrinally, the primary role of the sniper is to kill or disable individual enemy soldiers. He will normally do this from concealed positions up to a maximum effective rifle and optics range. He will also acquire targets beyond the range or capability of his rifle, for engagement by supporting arms. A secondary role for the sniper is the gathering of information on enemy activities and the provision of surveillance. Without question, the sniper's skills and application of optical devices, surveillance and silent movement techniques make him an outstanding reconnaissance asset. There are occasions when the sniper may prove more valuable for the intelligence he reports than for the target he interdicts.

To accomplish his role, the sniper will be employed in all types of conflict and all operations of war by day or by night in the following tasks:

• destroying enemy performing identifiably important functions, such as commanders, forward observers and reconnaissance patrols
• destroying enemy identified or selected by intelligence sources
• destroying selected enemy and other targets on his own initiative
• destroying enemy snipers (counter-sniping)

• observing and reporting on enemy dispositions and activities
• acquiring targets for engagement by combat-support weapons
• assisting in the coordination of friendly-force operations by virtue of his surveillance capabilities

The function of the sniper in an internal security scenario is to dominate the area of operations by delivery of selective, aimed fire against specific targets as authorized by local orders or instructions.

Below: Camouflage that suits the terrain and conditions helps these US Navy SEALS observe a target area undetected. Special forces snipers such as these have an important secondary role as forward observers and artillery spotters/forward air controllers.

Within this capacity some distinctive tasks which may be assigned to snipers include:

• engaging dissidents involved in such activities as hijacking, kidnapping and hostage-taking
• engaging dissident snipers as opportunity targets or as part of a deliberate clearing operation
• covertly occupying concealed positions to observe selected areas
• recording and reporting all suspicious activity in an area of observation

Below: The sniper's assistant (always a trained sniper himself) has more than a spotting role. In a tight spot he can cover the sniper's retreat and provide distracting or harassing fire.

• providing protection for other elements of the controlling forces including auxiliaries such as firemen and repair crews

Substitute the word 'criminal' for 'dissident' in this last passage, and these tasks describe many, indeed most, of the those carried out by police snipers as well.

A British army 'Skill At Arms' pamphlet, published in 1990, encapsulated the sniper thus: 'An infantry soldier who is an expert marksman and observer with the ability to locate an enemy, however well concealed, then stalk up or lie in wait to kill him with one round. He is able to observe, interpret and accurately report enemy movement. He can observe without being observed – kill without being being killed.'

These are broader and more demanding job descriptions, however, than the man carrying an issue sniper rifle in the Russian, Israeli or even French infantry might recognise. While individuals in those armies may well be capable of this range of work and will have the fieldcraft to carry it out, their mission is more often to act as an extension of a section or platoon's firepower. They will reach out with aimed, accurate fire beyond the effective range of the infantry assault rifle, concentrating on high-value, high-threat targets such as gun crews, mortars, vehicles and artillery (especially their sighting systems). They will carry this out as part of a general tactical plan, but will not operate independently of their immediate unit. As such, rather than being full-fledged snipers in the modern sense, they continue the tradition of the skirmisher and the marksman begun in the late eighteenth and early nineteenth centuries. Their kit (semi-automatic rather than more accurate bolt-action sniper rifles) reflects this difference in doctrine.

WHO'S IN CHARGE?

The modern sniper doesn't work alone, but as part of a two-man sniping team. Both are fully qualified in their trade, and rotate weapons and roles as sniper and spotter/observer – as often as half an hour or at most hourly – once they are in position in their hide. For the sake of military protocol, however, one of the team is 'officially' designated the sniper and team leader. The designated observer's share of the team-work is no less important – he may well be the more experienced of the two, as accurate range-finding and wind-judging are subtle matters, calling for much practice in extremely varied conditions. The observer will have all or some of the following tasks:

- obtaining and preparing any special gear, such as night-vision aids, navigational tools, and mission specific items
- leading (that is, navigating) the sniper cross-country before the real 'stalk' under full camouflage

- maintaining and carrying a full- or semi-automatic rifle or carbine (for defensive fire in emergency and covering while in the hide)
- following the sniper during the stalk and the exfiltration and hiding of any tracks
- helping to prepare and build the hide
- estimating ranges in consultation with the sniper
- estimating wind speed and direction with the sniper
- drawing up range cards (which act as a record of the operation as well as a guide to the terrain under observation)
- observing the designated sector with the spotting scope (usually 20x power)
- locating and distinguishing target indicators
- assigning priority to identified targets
- 'marking' shots – that is, telling the sniper if his shot has hit the target and, if not, where it did fall, so that his aim or sights can be adjusted to ensure a hit
- recording information observed and events as they occur
- communicating with other teams by radio
- operating any diversionary devices (e.g. smoke, white phosphorus)
- destroying the site when abandoning the hide

How the observer should be armed is a moot point. Some believe a scoped, accurized semi-automatic rifle such as the M14/M21 or Galil is the ideal weapon for back-up. More often, observers follow the advice of US Marine sniper and sniper instructor Sergeant Brian Poor in taking an assault rifle or carbine, and preferably one with a grenade launcher attached:

An example of the value of instantaneous, high-volume fire response took place during the third night of the ground war in Kuwait [during Operation Desert Storm]. STA Platoon 3/9 was traveling in three HMMWV's [light vehicles] though a fruit orchard near Kuwait International

Galil Sniper

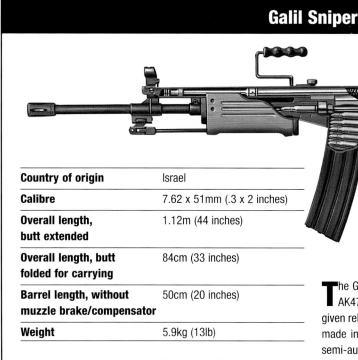

Country of origin	Israel
Calibre	7.62 x 51mm (.3 x 2 inches)
Overall length, butt extended	1.12m (44 inches)
Overall length, butt folded for carrying	84cm (33 inches)
Barrel length, without muzzle brake/compensator	50cm (20 inches)
Weight	5.9kg (13lb)

• Folding metal shoulder stock; fitted synthetic butt pad; wooden fore-end
• Any 25.4mm (1-inch) telescopic sight can be fitted to the generic mount, offset to the left and attached to a side rail; issue weapon features 6 x • 40 Nimrod scope
• Gas-operated self-loading
• Detachable 20-round box magazine

The Galil is an Israeli-made upgrade of the Soviet Kalashnikov AK47 assault rifle and is illustrated in its standard form. Data given relates to the Sniper variant, although some models are also made in 5.56 x 45mm. Both variants are selective fire – full or semi-automatic from a closed bolt. They have heavy match barrels fitted with a muzzle brake, a two-stage trigger, an integral bipod (attached to the gas block), adjustable cheek-piece and rubber recoil pad. This is not a perfect sniper's rifle – not suitable for a surgical shot – but is manageable and dependable.

M16/M203

Country of origin	United States	Overall length	1.12m (44 inches)
Calibre	5.56mm (.223 inches) M16, 40mm (1.57in) M203	Barrel length	84cm (33 inches)
		Weight	5.9kg (13lb)

Airport. The orchard was heavily fortified with bunkers, dug-in armored vehicles and concertina wire, but appeared to be abandoned. Our orders were to push through and seize the airport. We were engaged by an [Iraqi] RPK machine gun firing from a bunker 20 yards [18m] away. The machine gunner only got off about 15 rounds before he was killed by a high volume of automatic M16 fire directed at the muzzle flashes by myself and other observers. Would scoped M14s have worked? Certainly not as quickly. The gunner was dead three seconds after he pulled his trigger. Had he lived five seconds, I most likely

would have been hit, as his last couple of rounds passed inches from my head.

A sniper observer should carry an M16 with M203 grenade launcher attached. If you want two sniper weapons firing, then send two sniper teams, but do not make a sniper team's already very dangerous job worse by sending them out without an effective automatic weapon to protect themselves.

Current thinking in Britain and the USA seems to be that, in line regiments sniper, teams should be attached to the battalion in their own specialised platoon rather than directed as dispersed teams at company or platoon level. This means that they can operate semi-independently in a shooting and/or scouting capacity over a relatively wide area, as need arises, in any part of the battalion's sector –

Below: A USMC sniper shows off his skills with the M40 in front of his comrades during Operation 'Desert Shield' in Saudi Arabia. Variants of this 1960s rifle will be in Marine service well into the 21st century.

and whether the need is perceived by the team on the ground or by the unit commander acting on received intelligence. The sniper platoon in the US Marine Corps and US army light infantry divisions operates under the S2 intelligence officer or S3 operations officer.

The advantage of this centralised arrangement is that the sniper platoon will be commanded by a fellow sniper, will have its own dedicated training programme, will have a representative voice on the battalion staff, and so should be integrated into all battalion operations. As John Plaster comments:

Consolidation affords great flexibility in combat, allowing the battalion to concentrate or disperse the snipers to fit the situation and the mis-

Below: This LAV (Light Armoured Vehicle) may seem fearsome, but its aerials, sensors and vision devices can all be destroyed by a knowledgeable sniper, rendering them tactically useless.

sion. For instance, all snipers can be focused along one enemy avenue or approach, massed within one company's area if the terrain best suits sniping, or split evenly with three sniper teams attached to each company or one team for each line platoon. They can also run independent, battalion controlled operations.

The assumption here, of course, is that the battalion will be operating on some kind of 'conventional' battlefield where enemy and friendly lines are clearly drawn. But in the latter part of the twentieth century, standing armies were being called on to conduct 'peacekeeping' and 'low intensity' operations against guerrilla forces and rogue states, where there are often no 'front lines' as such, and which called for tactics and organisations nearer to those developed by Special Forces.

Special Forces generally operate both more covertly and in smaller units than conventional arms – as in the four-man troop of the British Special Air Service (SAS), or the platoon of the US Army Rangers. SAS troops are constructed from specialists appropriate to the operation, which may or may not require a sniper, but the regiment is small enough and flexible enough to mix and match men to form a suitable team. That will, as far as possible, rehearse the operation in detail. Members of platoon-size units that specialise in ambush and raiding need to know one another intimately, and so a sniper team is permanently attached to Ranger units. The snipers' standards of training, degree of readiness, and effectiveness in combat then depend largely on the imagination and awareness of a battalion commander, which may not be as concentrated or enthusiastic as a dedicated sniper platoon leader's.

However, though peacetime doctrine will state one thing, to paraphrase General Montgomery, no battle plan survives intact once troops have crossed their start line. John Plaster comments drily on the reality that in time of war 'any military organization can be dramatically changed to fit the circumstances ... When the bullets start flying, what matters is only

what works.' Adrian Gilbert quotes an officer in the British Parachute Regiment who supported the centralised system of a sniper platoon within the battalion, but had to put up with the slightly surreal rigidity of the military system:

I was very much of the opinion that snipers should be lodged with the intelligence cell but should work directly to the battalion CO, and not to a company commander or the intelligence officer. The problem was that there was no establishment for a sniping platoon within the battalion. But snipers had to 'belong' to somebody, and at one point our snipers were drummers – that's not uncommon – and what then happened was that somebody who could play a drum became a sniper – which isn't necessarily the best qualification to become a sniper! And we had some snipers, men who were good shots, who had to learn to play the drums, which again was lunatic.

When war in the Falklands became inevitable, however, a sniper platoon was rapidly formed, and served too as a cadre of musketry instructors to the rest of the regiment.

IN THE FIELD

Snipers can be deployed to deal with a variety of targets and reconnaissance tasks, in a broad range of fighting environments, depending on tactical need and whether their unit is advancing or withdrawing.

The roster of a sniper's targets will remain much the same whatever his unit's circumstances: enemy commanders; weapons crews; sighting and surveillance systems (from a tank driver's vision block to a radar antenna); enemy snipers; and targets of opportunity. In an advance, the sniper will set about such items in order to jeopardise the enemy's defensive manoeuvres and responses; in a withdrawal or retreat, destroying the same targets will slow the enemy's advance. Successful sniper fire can both blind and emasculate an enemy, and is especially valuable when troops are moving into the open from cover, whether in assault or to create or reach a defensive position.

Strategically important infrastructure makes particularly inviting sniper targets. Crossroads, passes in hill country, bridges, airfields, railways, radio and telephone installations can be defended or interdicted with sniper fire. In such applications lightweight .50BMG rifles, which can destroy an aircraft, disable a tank or wreck a radio transmission mast are especially useful. Even the standard 7.62mm/.308Win-calibre sniper rifle is effective against armour, given that most tank drivers and commanders tend to drive 'head up' rather than behind vision blocks or buttoned up, for the perfectly sensible reason that the need to see the battlefield usually outweighs the risk of injury or death. Even a vision block can be splintered and made opaque. Besides, the hull and turret of a modern main battle tank are littered with infrared, laser, and optical sighting, ranging and guidance systems as well as radio antennae. Destroying any of these is well within a sniper's capability and will promptly cripple the fat metal beast, and may render it useless. A .50BMG round can smash one of its tracks and immobilise it to boot, so it can't even be used as a self-propelled battering ram.

Fighting in built-up areas (FIBUA) presents a special challenge to military snipers, although this is home territory for most police marksmen. FIBUA has been part of Western military doctrine since the Allied armies, learning on the hoof, had to hack their way street by street through European cities in the latter days of World War II. But the need for an intimate understanding of urban warfare has increased exponentially as post-modern conflicts have involved infantry more and more in peacekeeping and policing operations in cities. Where the population is largely hostile, and actively or passively supports a guerrilla faction, the sniper (in

Right: A patrol in Northern Ireland adopts low-profile movements in a known sniper zone. The middle soldier is himself equipped with a counter-sniper weapon, an FN assault rifle.

common with his colleagues on patrol) is at a daunting disadvantage: this is the enemy's ground, and he knows it instinctively. Thus he can make the most of dead ground that's invisible to the sniper, whose field of view is inevitably limited by buildings and by his location within a building in which he is hiding. True, the sniper has on his side an almost infinite number of potential hiding places and therefore every opportunity to mislead the enemy as to his actual whereabouts by creating 'dummy' positions. At the same time an enemy sniper can exploit exactly the same features of the urban landscape, so counter-sniping becomes an immense test of the soldier's powers of observation and patience.

For a sniper, movement in the city is a separate art from anything he may know or learn on an open battlefield. Putting him in place may involve setting up an apparently routine patrol that includes the sniper team. The pair can then 'mysteriously' vanish from the body of the patrol to take up their position. (A later seemingly routine patrol can pick them up in the same way when their tour is over.) When they drop away from that patrol, however, they may have to slip down a manhole into the sewers to make their way beneath the streets to the building they've chosen to hole up in. They may move under cover of smoke, or some other diversionary tactic. They may even go in disguise. They will rarely if ever go directly to their chosen destination: they may duck inside one building only in order to 'mousehole' their way to another several doors away in a terrace by breaking through intervening walls until they reach their selected hide.

Once there, they will set up well back from any windows. (The history of sniping is replete with tales of over-confident snipers who gave themselves away by poking barrels out of windows, letting the sun flash off their telescopes, or simply letting their muzzle flash be seen.) Or they may decide that chopping a hole in the exterior wall, like an old-fashioned arrow-slit, is the best option, especially if battle scars on the building they're in create a

'natural' camouflage for such a rent (it's not a tactic that will work on Fifth Avenue). Ideally, they'll find a handy table or bed or two so that they can observe and shoot from a prone position. Once in place, and readying themselves to shoot, they will have to bear in mind all the quaint and curious behaviours of winds in city streets. At least range-finding should not be a problem, given large-scale modern maps and satellite and aerial photographs from which to work.

MAKING A SNIPER

There are three skills a would-be sniper has to master before he can go out into the field: marksmanship, fieldcraft and tactics. He also has to be a particular, and not exactly common, kind of person. The more refined sniper-training courses are designed to weed out the wrong kind of characters or those who simply aren't bright enough or physically strong enough for the work. Some military arms and large police agencies use psychological

The trainee sniper learns shooting from a variety of positions including prone (non-shooting hand on rear sling swivel, rifle supported by object) and Hawkins (rifle supported by non-shooting hand), which is seen here.

and, inevitably, raise its overall standards in the field.

American instructors are plain-spoken about the toughness of their sniper schools. Captain Tim Hunter, a former officer in charge at the US Marine scout-sniper school at Quantico, Virginia, has explained:

> Our students are on the go all day long in a combination of field and classroom work. But they still have a lot of studying to do at night because they are tested the next day. And they also have written assignments. This is not a boot camp and we don't treat our students like recruits. They're already good Marines or they wouldn't be here. But we make the course stressful. Being a scout sniper is an extremely stressful business. The school shows us how a future scout sniper will act and react under pressure. If he can't handle that stress in a school situation, there is no way he will be able to cope with it on the battlefield ... If a Marine thinks he can come here and 'hot dog' his way through the school, he'll be out on his ear.

And Gunnery Sergeant Paul S. Herrmann, a former Non-Commissioned Officer in Charge of the school, has elaborated:

> We really stack the deck against the students. The most dangerous thing a sniper can face is another sniper, because a sniper knows just what to look for. Our students are facing two trained snipers [who are both instructors at the school, and] who act as observers during the stalk. The students are heading toward the observers, down a channelled area, from a known distance. They have a four-hour time limit in broad daylight.

screening as part of the selection for training, but it will ultimately be the way the candidate sniper responds to the course itself that shows if he has got what it takes. The US Marine Corps and US Army courses reckon to have a pass rate of about 40 per cent. The British Army awards sniper's badges to about one in five of those who start its courses. Those who either don't complete sniper courses or who don't pass all the tests are not regarded as failures, for they take valuable lessons back to their unit

Coming to within 200 yards [180m] of the observers, who have high-powered spotting scopes, the students must set up, fire a blank round at them, and then wait. If the observers can't see where the first shot came from, then the student fires again. If his position isn't spotted by then, the student has made a 'possible' on that stalk. That's very rare, especially in the first weeks. The other instructors and I pride ourselves on being good observers.

If you don't think there's a lot of stress involved, try crawling 800 yards [730m] through the brush, firing a shot, and before you get to fire the second round, being spotted by the observer because of some silly mistake. In a real situation, of course, the sniper would never come that close to a target. We believe if they can set up on us, with the deck really stacked up against them, they can set up on anyone.

Once qualified and assigned to a scout-sniper platoon in the US Marines (and the same goes for other snipers in other arms), the training continues in the form of exercises – and the possibility of a 'live' operation. Sergeant Craig T. Douglas, a former section leader in a sniper platoon, has said:

It takes desire, drive, and a lot of heart to be a Scout/Sniper. Operational commitments and tempos are very high-paced. The Marines here endure a lot of fatigue, both physically and mentally, and have to be able to remain proficient throughout. If you don't love living in the field getting dirty, cut up, moving in waist-deep swamps, getting in fistfights with bugs, and staying cold for weeks at a time then this isn't the job for you.

Field skills are just as important as being able to shoot well. The field skills of each platoon

Left: Royal Marine sniper trainees stalk the toughest target: a group of instructors who know every trick in the sniper's book. This scenario is deliberately more difficult than most likely combat situations, but success is a great confidence builder.

member must be far and above the abilities and knowledge of the average infantryman. Each must to be able to call in supporting arms and close air support. Because we use a variety of communications equipment, we have to be as good as any radio operator in the Marine Corps.

Once we gather the intelligence, we have to get it back to the unit we are supporting. It could be the security of a landing zone, whether the ground composition or obstacles will prohibit a landing, enemy aircraft in an area, or a surf or beach report to assist amphibious landings.

Regardless of the situation, if we can't get that information back, then we're no good out there. All we'll do is give away the battalion's intent. We're called Scout/Snipers because the scouting role comes first. If you get to take a shot or are shooting in support of a mission, that's all good and well, but the missions are primarily scout-based. We will take a shot in various situations, however, such as in support of light armored or amphibious assault vehicles when they roll up for a hard hit.

A cynic may be forgiven for wondering how much of Douglas's playing-down of the importance of marksmanship was strictly a public-relations ploy, designed to make the sniper look (for whatever unfathomable reason) like some kind of 'nice guy'. Since World War I it's been part of the sniper's job to gather intelligence, and that task may indeed occupy most of his time in the field – but it would never have arisen but for the sniper's expertise with a rifle. So it remains true that without that essential skill, and the scores to prove it, no one who wants to be a sniper – or a scout/sniper – gets onto a training course.

HOW TO HIT A TARGET

Anyone who has spent hours on a range shooting a rifle at long ranges – that is, anything beyond 365m (400 yards) – will have learned something of the essentials of sniping. For instance, he will be so famil-

iar with the basic techniques of accurate rifle shooting that they will have become instinctive. The USMC teaches (or, according to some, merely announces, without delving further) these as 'B-R-A-S-S', or: Breathe, Relax, Aim, Slack, Squeeze.

Whole books have been written on this sequence. The first and the last are possibly the most important. 'Breathe' means knowing that before firing you

get where you want to. The trick, then, is to learn how to take the shot as soon after holding the breath as possible, without 'snatching' it (pulling it off aim through haste). And here is the importance of relaxing. The more the shooter strains for the perfect sight picture, the tenser he becomes, the more likely he is to react by fighting the inevitable wobble in the rifle, and the more the rifle will proceed to wobble. So relaxing must come before being sure of the aim. 'Slack' simply means taking up first pressure on the trigger – moving it into the position where further pressure will let the shot break. 'Squeeze' refers to the ability to put pressure on the trigger in such a way that you don't put pressure on the rifle as well – in other words, making the trigger move back while remaining perfectly in line with the rifle, not pushing or pulling it in any other direction.

To do this successfully, the trigger finger has to be free of the stock, and the pad of the end joint should be touching the trigger. One technique for avoiding any sideways pressure while squeezing the trigger is to imagine you're trying to draw it in a dead straight line into the aiming eye. All these things have to be done in a very short time (though time seems to stretch under stress, to the shooter's advantage) and having made sure as far as possible that your body is positioned so that it too is not making you fight the rifle, that the sling is properly adjusted, that you've achieved a firm 'weld' between cheek and stock, and that you're able to deal with the inevitable rush of adrenalin that comes with getting a live target in your sights.

The sniper needs to know the idiosyncrasies of his rifle intimately. Civilian marksmanship competitions and military range work involve consistent shooting, shot after shot, and civilians have the convenience of being able to take sighting shots to check their zero and wind effects before starting to

should breathe in, to oxygenate the blood, then breathe out, and hold the breath. For about five or eight seconds you and the rifle will stay quite steady. Then, imperceptibly at first, the rifle will begin to wobble as oxygen is depleted from the bloodstream. In fact, the muzzle describes a tiny spiral, and it widens the longer the breath is held. The longer you stay in the aim, the less likely you are to hit the tar-

address the target that will count. What all this means is that serious target shooting is done with a rifle that's warmed up and whose barrel is, if ever so slightly, fouled from repeated firing. The sniper enjoys no such luxury, which adds some more subtlety to his complex existence, for a bullet behaves differently when shot from a clean, cold barrel (CCB), and that is what the sniper uses, unless he's in the kind of trouble he should have avoided.

It's critical then that the sniper learns how to predict the fall of a CCB shot. The first step in this process is to establish the shooter/rifle combination's ability to group shots. Dedicated sniper rifles are built to produce an inch or half-inch group – 1 or

Left: Cleanliness of the rifle, in this case an Accuracy International AW, the standard British sniper's weapon, is essential. This is especially important for the sniper, who above all needs consistency of shot between the range and the 'live' target.

Above: A Ukrainian SFOR sniper in Bosnia in 1998 takes aim with the Russian-made Dragunov SVD sniper rifle. The long barrel provides accuracy in still wind conditions but is unduly cumbersome for stalking.

0.5 minutes of angle (MOA) – at 91.5m (100 yards), measuring the group from the centre of each bullet hole. A shot will land on any point within that area purely by chance. Not all shooters are capable of shooting as accurately as their rifle, but a 1 MOA group should be the sniper's minimum standard, making a successful head shot feasible at 640m (700 yards). Once it's established where, relative to the point of aim, the rifle groups, the sights can be adjusted to ensure the bullets fall in a cluster around the point of aim. (This is 'zeroing'.) A CCB shot should fall within that cluster, but some combinations of rifle, shooter or ammunition will always produce a CCB outside it.

Dragunov SVD Sniper Rifle

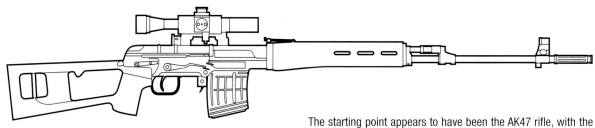

Country of origin	Russia
Calibre	7.62 x 54mm (.3 x 2.13 inches) rimmed (using specially designed steel-core bullets)
Overall length	1.22m (48.13 inches)
Barrel length	62cm (24.5 inches)
Weight with scope	4.3kg (9lb 8oz)

• Laminated-wood stock, ventilated handguards and open 'anatomical' style butt; later versions with synthetic materials
• 4 x 24 PSO-1 telescope, with infrared detector; reticle illuminated for low-light use; iron sights for back up
• Gas-operated, self-loading
• Detachable 10-shot box magazine

This project started in 1958 with the intention of developing a replacement sniper weapon for the Mosin-Nagant M91/30.

The starting point appears to have been the AK47 rifle, with the design stretched to accommodate the older 7.62 x 54R Mosin Nagant cartridge, and a short-stroke gas piston to reduce the effect of reloading on accuracy. The weapon is semi-automatic only, and in the event of a gas system malfunction, should operate as a straight pull-bolt action. After protracted modifications in competition with other designers (including Kalashnikov), the Dragunov was adopted by the Red Army in 1963.

During its occupation of Afghanistan the Red Army found the SVD was awkward to carry and impossible to use within its BMP armoured personnel carriers, and commissioned a version of the SVD with a folding stock. The result, designated the SVDS (*Snayperskaya Vintovka Dragunova, Skladnaya*), was completed in 1994. This has an overall length of 1.13m (44.75 inches), folding down to 87.5cm (34.5 inches), with a heavier, chromium-plated 56.5cm (22.25-inch) barrel, a new conical muzzle brake with teardrop-shaped slots, a pistol grip and handguards made of black thermosetting fibreglass-reinforced polyamide. It weighs slightly more than the SVD at 4.6kg (10lb 3oz). Both versions are in production and in service.

Given that in the field or on the street the sniper's 'one shot – one kill' requirement will in principle be made with a CCB, such a problem has to be addressed. The solution is to fire one CCB shot, then clean the rifle, and fire another CCB round without adjusting the sights – and repeat the process until you have a 5- or 10-round group on the target. The sights should then be adjusted so that this group – not one fired from a warm barrel – becomes the standard for the zero. All other things being equal, the one shot the sniper has to guarantee to be a hit will then find its mark. There is another lesson to be learned from this exercise: the sniper must keep his weapon clean and cool!

Semi-automatic weapons throw an extra peculiarity on top of the CCB effect, adding to the distinctiveness of the first shot, and the quirk has helped to make the bolt-action rifle the weapon of choice for the fully fledged modern sniper. The first shot from a semi-automatic weapon is always slightly 'off' compared to following shots. This is because that first round is loaded into the chamber when the rifle is cocked manually, an action that lacks the far greater energy imparted when the recoil spring compresses in response to the gases released by a round firing. And so, in turn, the spring then expands and the bolt slams forward much more vigorously as it loads the following round. The second and following rounds will be thoroughly seated (even slightly distorted) in the chamber and, most important, consistently so. The difference in the position of the automatically chambered round may be as little as .127mm (.005 inches), but that's enough to affect the group on the target, as the propellant in the cartridge will burn at greater pressure, produce higher muzzle velocity, and alter the bullet's trajectory. At sniping distances that may make the difference between a hit and a miss. With a manually operated rifle, the more precise mechanics of the bolt action create a greater consistency in chambering the round, even with a warm barrel.

THE WIND AND THE RAIN

Even an accomplished target shooter, out in the field, will have to learn a whole new set of skills in order to be an effective sniper. A target shooter

knows how far he's shooting, because someone's measured the distance between his firing point and the range butts with considerable care. In the field, he'll have to decide, with the help of his spotter and by various methods, the distance between himself and his prey, and he needs his calculation to be extremely accurate. On the rifle range, flags at measured intervals tell him what the wind is doing all the way to the target. A sniper won't have that kind of help, no matter how merciful his enemy, and he'll have to learn new ways to read the wind and judge his shot. Rifle ranges are flat and the targets don't walk about. But a sniper has to know what will happen to his bullet when he's

Below: Sniper training emphasises real world conditions. This Italian Caribinieri sniper is firing from a position that simulates a window ledge, his most likely firing position in a terrorist or hostage situation. His weapon is an Anschutz .22 Carbine.

SIG SSG550 Sniper Rifle

Country of origin	Switzerland
Calibre	5.6mm – 5.56 x 45mm (.223 x 1.78 inches)
Overall length, stock extended	1.13m (44.5 inches)
Overall length, folded	90.5cm (35.75 inches)
Barrel length	52.8cm (20.875 inches)
Weight	7.1kg (15lb 10oz)

- Heavy-duty shock-resistant plastic stock; fully adjustable butt; bipod
- Mount for telescopic and night sights; issue sight is 4x Kern
- Gas-operated semi-automatic
- Detachable 20-round transparent-plastic box magazine

Based on the immensely durable and accurate Swiss Army Sturmgewehr 90 (SG550) assault rifle designed by SIG, the SSG (*Scharfschutzengewehr* – sharpshooting rifle) 550 is unusual in being built around the 5.6mm round. A heavy target barrel and adjustable double-pull trigger increase accuracy.

firing at any given angle uphill or down, and he's unlikely to have much opportunity to choose the ground over which he shoots. He has to know how much 'lead' to put on a target if it's moving, and be able to judge how fast it's going, to boot. These skills will have been learned, probably over years, as a matter of course by a deerstalker, a big-game hunter, or a farmer's son intent on protecting lambs and fowl from foxes and other predatory mammals. A candidate sniper starts with a major advantage if he has a background of hunting or vermin control but, if he doesn't have that, he must be smart and quick enough to learn these things from scratch.

There are a number of ways to estimate range, and it's not unusual to use more than one of them and compare the results. Using laser range-finders is the most accurate, but it's not always safe to beam visible or infrared light around a battlefield or behind enemy lines, so all these techniques have to be learned, and practised assiduously, because accurate range-finding comes only with long experience. And knowing by experience how far one is from a distant object on a clear day may not always help when conditions are less than perfect, or even subtly different.

Points the sniper has to take into account when judging distance by eye include:

• A regularly shaped object such as a house or truck appears closer than one with an irregular outline, such as a tree or a copse.

• A target that contrasts sharply in colour or shape with its background appears to be closer than it actually is. But a man standing among large rocks, trees or tall buildings will seem farther away.

• A target that's only partly visible seems farther away than it actually is.

• The more detail that's visible on a target, the closer it appears. The detail may be apparent only because of atmospheric conditions.

• When the sun is behind the observer, the target appears to be closer.

• When the sun is behind the target, the target is more difficult to see, appearing to be farther away.

• Flat terrain such as water, sand, snow or the line of sight down a railroad track fools the observer into underestimating the range to distant targets.

• If the target is viewed down a hill or across a depression, it appears farther away. By the same token, looking uphill at a target makes it seem closer.

Once all these factors have been taken into account, the sniper team creates a range card. The legendary Carlos Hathcock once explained to police snipers what that involved, and the importance to snipers of record-keeping in general:

When you move into an area, move slowly – slow, deliberate movement, observing everything

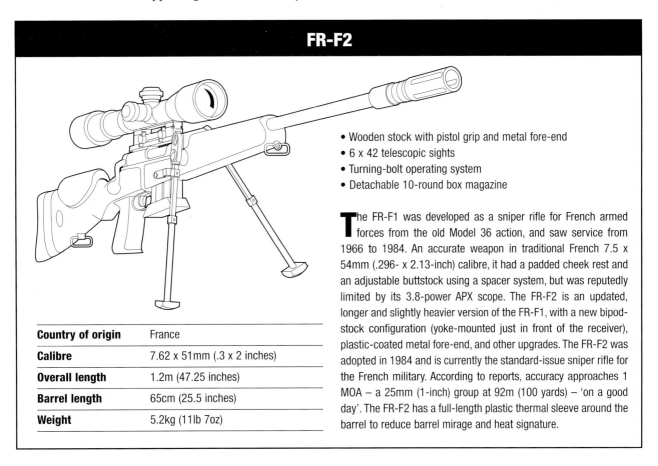

FR-F2

• Wooden stock with pistol grip and metal fore-end
• 6 x 42 telescopic sights
• Turning-bolt operating system
• Detachable 10-round box magazine

The FR-F1 was developed as a sniper rifle for French forces from the old Model 36 action, and saw service from 1966 to 1984. An accurate weapon in traditional French 7.5 x 54mm (.296- x 2.13-inch) calibre, it had a padded cheek rest and an adjustable buttstock using a spacer system, but was reputedly limited by its 3.8-power APX scope. The FR-F2 is an updated, longer and slightly heavier version of the FR-F1, with a new bipod-stock configuration (yoke-mounted just in front of the receiver), plastic-coated metal fore-end, and other upgrades. The FR-F2 was adopted in 1984 and is currently the standard-issue sniper rifle for the French military. According to reports, accuracy approaches 1 MOA – a 25mm (1-inch) group at 92m (100 yards) – 'on a good day'. The FR-F2 has a full-length plastic thermal sleeve around the barrel to reduce barrel mirage and heat signature.

Country of origin	France
Calibre	7.62 x 51mm (.3 x 2 inches)
Overall length	1.2m (47.25 inches)
Barrel length	65cm (25.5 inches)
Weight	5.2kg (11lb 7oz)

know exactly where he is talking about and you don't have to search the whole area for the bad guy. If you are watching a building, number the windows and you'll know exactly where the observer spots the suspect when he calls out 'window three'.

Keep a data book with the information that concerns your rifle. Know how many shots have been fired through that barrel. If you wear out a barrel on the range, it would be nice to know that you need a new barrel before you have to make that one well-aimed shot for real.

Log books contain the basic information and record of each situation you have been involved in. Keep a record of Who, What, Where, When, Conditions, Wind, Range, Shots Fired, Situation and Location. The information is invaluable later to your intelligence people or command post. You are in the best position to see what is going on.

Understanding the effects of wind on a bullet is, in principle, simple enough. The farther a bullet flies, the slower it gets, and the less energy it retains. Wind has an exponentially greater effect on a bullet's behaviour at the long ranges that are the sniper's forte. A wind blowing at 24km/h (15mph) (a strong breeze) will make a 7.62mm/.308Win bullet drift 11.5cm (4.5 inches) from the target at a mere 183m (200 yards) – enough to miss a head shot if it's not taken into account. At 550m (600 yards) the difference between an unadjusted aiming point and bullet impact is a full 1.2m (48 inches). Clearly snipers need to compensate for effects like this, and that means, first of all, knowing how to judge wind speed.

A simple method taught to every novice soldier is to look at the environment. Winds up to 5km/h (3mph) make smoke drift, but are otherwise virtu-

you can see. Analyse the terrain and know how you're going to get there and how you're going to get back. Never get into a hurry if you don't have to. After you occupy your firing position, you have to sweep the area in front visually, making sure there is nothing that will endanger or affect you or your partner. Scan the area from left to right, then right to left. Note the bushes, trash cans, trees, cars and so on.

You and your observer set up a range card so that you know exactly what is out there by writing down each prime point. You number each obstacle and point so that you each know what to shift to if a number is called out. When the observer says, 'Section A, position 2,' you

ally undetectable. A light breeze on the face is a wind around 5–8km/h (3–5mph). Trees start to move when the wind is running between 8–13km/h (5–8mph). When dust lifts from the ground and paper swirls around, wind speed is about 13–19km/h (8–12mph), and when small trees sway it's at around 19–24km/h (12–15mph). Not a lot of which is helpful if you are trying to set up a shot in a disused dockyard full of abandoned cranes and rusting containers, but no trees, no smoke, and only soggy waste paper on the ground.

At long ranges the 20x-power spotting scope comes into its own, for it can detect the effects of heat on the air, which creates a mirage. This looks like moving wrinkles in the image seen through the scope. Their ripples will follow the direction of the wind, or come straight up from the ground (a 'boil-ing' mirage) if there's no wind (or if the wind is blowing fore or aft of the shooter, in which case it can be disregarded). Large ripples indicate a slow wind; smaller ones show a wind at speed. Learning to judge what these mean in terms of actual wind speed is once more a matter of practice, experience and acuity. The method is little use for winds running at over 19km/h (12mph) in any case, for the movement of the ripples becomes almost too fast to analyse. A simple solution to these problems is to move, if possible, to a position that's directly up- or down-wind of the target area. To add to the sniper's

Below: Estimating range and wind direction is one of the sniper's many skills. Changes in wind speed, direction and temperature all affect bullet drop and divergence from the aiming point. This terrain offers many clues for the observant sniper.

troubles, he has to remember that the mirage effect actually shifts the image of the target he sees through the scope from its true location. He has to judge where his target really is, as distinct from where it appears to be.

If this all seems tricky enough, calculations about the wind are further complicated by the variable nature of air currents. Even on a flat range – target shooters know from reading indicator flags – winds can seem calm at either end but be gusty in the middle. Add in the effects of trees, changes in elevation of ground, the funnelling effects of canyons, road or railway cuttings (whether through earth or forest) and buildings, and compensating the aim for wind becomes a subtle process indeed. In cities, wind will move in different directions at different heights between buildings. Watching the wind is a sniper's constant duty. Having once judged the speed and direction of the wind at regular positions along the field of fire, he has to keep a sharp eye open for changes. Over long ranges, the only practical route is to average out the effects over a series of ranges, and adjust the rifle sights accordingly.

Climate and weather affect a bullet's behaviour too. High temperatures produce less resistance and increase the velocity of the bullet, which makes the bullet strike higher on the target, and low temperatures do the opposite. Humidity produces more resistance, which lowers the bullet's striking point too. These effects too have to be factored in to the final sight setting, or into the extent the sniper decides to 'aim off' target to compensate for them.

THERE AND BACK

Even if a trainee sniper is a master shot with a rifle, he still has to learn how to make his way to his area of operations, set up a hide, and – having made his

Right: Royal Marines in their ghillie suits stalk through a wetland area. Snipers must be aware of changing terrain as they move in order to avoid being silhouetted against a contrasting background.

Left: The best ghillie suits can conceal a sniper from an enemy only a few feet away and are as naturalistic as the camouflage of a tree moth. Each suit is as individual as its creator, whose life indeed depends on its effectiveness.

kill – get back to his rendezvous point or behind his own lines in one piece. He has to know how to read a map as if it were a three-dimensional model of the earth, how to navigate, how to choose a position at which to hide, and how to become virtually invisible while doing all these things. This, in short, is fieldcraft.

A sniper can't do anything very useful if he's spotted, and the essentials of remaining undetected are cover, concealment, and camouflage. Instructor Richard Boucher defines cover like this:

Cover is the protection of the sniper from small arms fire. Cover can be natural such as a hiding place behind a rock or it can be man-made, such as a tank. The enemy may know where the sniper is located but can not hit the sniper with small arms fire. Cover, while protection from small arms fire, does not mean the sniper is undetected and when under cover the sniper can not complete his mission. The sniper must come out of cover to 'see' the target and engage and once out the enemy now has the capability of detecting

Below: White camouflage suits are the obvious choice for snowy winter terrain, but a mix of white and woodland camouflage often gives the best concealment in forested terrain such as seen in this Korean War photograph.

Above: A sniper's hide can make use of both natural and man-made objects, in this case a vehicle. While he is well camouflaged, his rifle violates at least two of the 'Five Ss' of concealment. Camouflage paint and use of the shadows would assist greatly.

and engaging the sniper. This means that the sniper must rely on concealment.

Concealment, says Boucher, is protection from observation. It may be natural concealment – such as bushes, grass and shadows – or artificial, with the sniper using materials such as burlap and camouflage nets. Artificial concealment can also involve moving natural materials from their original locations. Successful use of concealment materials, both natural and artificial, may depend on the season, weather and light.

Camouflage is what the sniper uses to mask the colour, outline, or texture of himself and his equip-ment. Vegetation or other materials native to the area provide natural camouflage. Boucher recommends making 60–70 per cent of camouflage natural, only 30–40 per cent artificial: 'Man-made substances will always appear, under scrutiny, to be man-made,' he says. 'The secret to camouflage is to never draw the attention of the enemy and create a reason for the enemy to "inspect with close scrutiny" your position. Once that occurs, you will be observed due to target indicators.'

Under 'target indicators' he includes tactile give-aways, such as 'cut branches from hide construction or partial clearing of a fire lane, trip wires or warning devices ... Closer to your site would be poorly concealed hide edges, equipment left outside the hide, litter,' and so on. A sniper needs to remember that his enemy can smell, too: latrine trenches have to be well covered, food should be taken that can be eaten without cooking, rifle-cleaning solvents should be the ones used by the enemy. Who also has ears: moving soundlessly as possible is *de rigueur*, and anything that might rattle should be taped into silence. Messages between team members should be by hand signal, and radio contact has to be made through pre-set signals using the radio squelch button. Sound carries best at night, and then noise of any kind has to be reduced to zero. David Reed has a few dry comments on nocturnal communications in a sniper team:

Forget birdcalls. Unless your enemy is a bunch of idiots they will know your signals are not birds chirping. Most birds call in the early morning and evening. They do not call each other in the middle of the night. Owls hoot, but how many owls do you hear? Are they native to the area? Owls stick to one area their entire lives. If you have one near your house you will hear him every now and then. If the enemy has been in an area for several weeks without hearing an owl, and suddenly they hear two of them hooting back and forth they are not going to think it's two owls. Any noise you make will be assumed a threat and fired upon. Forget cowboy movie tricks, your enemy has probably seen a few westerns too.

When it comes to what the enemy might see, the standard fieldcraft drill is to remember, and act on, the 'Five Ss': Shape, Shine, Shadow, Silhouette and Spacing.

Essentially this means that straight lines – a sure sign of a human presence – should be avoided, down to covering rifle barrels with scrim; anything reflective or bright should be made dull, from the distinctive human face (camouflaged with greasepaint) to the heels of boots, and anything smooth should be made rough or crinkly; movement should be within

Right: This US Marine demonstrates the basic construction of a ghillie suit. Camouflage material is not added to the front of this example so as to aid crawling. The integral hood, rather than the more usual camouflaged helmet, is also noteworthy.

be within shadows wherever possible, and creating shadows, even on the body, should be avoided; keep away from crests and skylines; and if there are more than two members in a sniper team, they should keep random distances from one another. The sniper has to be prepared to move slowly, indirectly, and inconsistently to his objective. The enemy – for trainee snipers, that's the instructors – will notice not only human movement, but sudden flights (and their alarm calls) of birds or animals, odd movements of plants and bushes, and so on. Camouflage has to be appropriate to the local terrain, and of the right colour, and may have to be changed frequently so that the sniper always blends into his background. Grass and saplings grow up toward the sun: a patch of strangely flattened vegetation will instantly raise suspicion and if – even more remarkably – it's seen to move, it will draw fire.

MOVING AND HIDING

The sniper's best hope of remaining invisible when moving – 'on the stalk' – in grass and woodland is his ghillie suit. Candidate snipers have to make their own – not to improve their needlework and social standing as New Men, but on the same principle whereby paratroopers pack their own 'chutes. Your life depends on it, so any mistakes in the making should be your own, with no one else to blame if it doesn't work properly. The suit, which can take up to 50 hours to put together, was first created by gamekeepers (ghillies) in the Scottish Highlands in the nineteenth century. Some say they were made to

Below: Ghillie suits often give the sniper the comic appearance of 'Swamp Thing', but the more outlandish they are, the better they work. These men are German paratroopers from Fallschirmjägerbatailon 314, armed with H&K G3-A3 ZF rifles.

combat poachers, but deer, as any stalker knows, are sharp-eyed and shy, and deeply suspicious of people. A ghillie suit is hot and heavy: a set of camouflage-pattern overalls, with a tough canvas front and extra patches on knees and elbows to ease the pain of crawling, it is covered in netting (to which vegetation can be tied or 'garnished'), with hundreds of burlap or hessian strips (stained in natural colours) tied into its back and edges, to break up the distinctive human outline. One commentator described the finished articles as 'scarecrow suits Worzel Gummidge would envy'; another described seeing a sniper rise from nearby grass as 'a bizarre apparition, part scarecrow, part zombie'. But sur-

Above: Trainee Caribinieri snipers check the targets on the firing range. Only the most exceptional shots graduate as snipers in military Special Forces or police anti-terrorist/hostage rescue teams.

viving on the modern battlefield has never been too elegant a matter.

In cities, various shades of grey seem to make the most effective personal camouflage, and here the occasional straight line and smooth surface will blend into the hard, urban background. White suits, usually looser than standard uniform to break up the human profile, are worn against full snow or ice, but where there is ground snow but none on the trees, a woodland camouflage jacket and white trousers do

Above: A Royal Marine shows how application of camouflage scrim can break up the bulky outline of an SA80 rifle with a high-power scope. The SA80 is not a sniper's rifle as such, but it is used in the training course for British snipers.

much to foil an enemy's preconceived idea of what a man should look like. In desert country, a ghillie suit is usually impracticable, and little can be done to blur a man's shape against sand: use of colour in the camouflage suit pattern, and whatever local vegetation there is (if any) are the sniper's best hopes. In any terrain, spray paint can be used to reduce the contrast of issue uniform with the actual environment. And as much attention has to be paid to smudging the rifle's distinctive shape. When on the stalk, weapons (apart from sidearms) are usu-ally taken down, packed, and dragged behind or beside the sniper.

The actual route, candidate snipers learn, has to be carefully plotted, using maps and aerial photographs if available. It should be taken in short stages, using all available cover, and a variety of styles of crawling if need be. This reduces the sniper's exposure to prying eyes, and offers opportunities for rest, for checking progress and position, and for gathering intelligence. The return route has

to be equally carefully planned, for it's a golden rule of sniping never to go back the way you came in. You never know what clues you may, however inadvertently, have left to your passage. And if you've hit a major target, the enemy will be extra vigilant and vengeful.

Building a hide calls on all the techniques of cover, concealment and camouflage that the stalk does, with the additional consideration that, being immobile, it's more prone to detection. What kind of hide is constructed depends on the mission. It may be a 'hasty' hide, little more than a rapid adaptation of the local terrain to provide cover and concealment before a shot is taken and the sniper moves on. Keeping the rifle barrel out of sight to hide muzzle flash is still a prime consideration, and damping the earth or laying damp cloth below the muzzle will reduce the chances of dust or leaves being kicked up and giving the position away. A long surveillance mission, on the other hand, can involve building an elaborate shelter (a job most safely done at night) with an overhead cover – strong enough for a man to stand on, and as unnoticeable as possible – and observation/firing loopholes. The front of such a hide should be made bulletproof, and spoil should be carted away as far as practicable. The hide should be big enough to allow the team some movement, to exercise stiff muscles.

Perhaps most important, it should not be set up in a position that is altogether obviously 'ideal' for sniping. The enemy will no doubt have checked out all such positions and will be watching them. If the sniper team can mislead the enemy into thinking any fire is coming from such a position while holding a less obvious, equally useful, and perfectly concealed one themselves, they will have done their job. Of course it's possible to try second-guessing your opponent, and deliberately choosing the 'obvious' position on the grounds that it's altogether too obvious. But a cautious anti-sniper policy would triple-guess that kind of thinking, and take out a mad minute occasionally to saturate such positions with fire, 'just in case'. Better to be clever than too clever.

REALISM AND DEATH

Even the most highly regarded sniper training courses can't entirely prepare their students for the real thing. One US Army sniping instructor at Fort Benning, Georgia, has been quoted as saying that 'how a sniper will react after he takes out his first human target is completely unpredictable. Training cannot truly prepare them for having to shoot an unarmed person or political target ... You get a feel for the force a bullet can inflict on paper targets and iron maidens, but until you see it through optics at 10 power, you don't know how it will affect you.'

Other sniper trainers try to prepare their students by making the targets as realistic as possible (a technique also used in World War II by the veteran expert Clifford Shore). Carlos Hathcock commented on this problem: 'If you are going to train to shoot people, then targets should look like people. Few suspects dress up to look like bull's eyes. When you look through that scope, the first things that jump out on you are the eyes. You see a living human being in your sights. I teach with targets that show life-size faces.'

Chuck Kramer, who trained Israeli snipers, went one step further:

I made the targets as human as possible. I changed the standard firing targets to full-size, anatomically correct figures because no Syrian runs around with a big white square on his chest with numbers on it. I put clothes on these targets and polyurethane heads. I cut up a cabbage and put catsup onto it and put it back together. I said, 'When you look through that scope, I want you to see a head blowing up.'

The British Parachute Regiment took even that a step further, as one instructor explained to Adrian Gilbert:

Right: This Italian 5th Alpine Regiment sniper demonstrates an almost perfect matching of camouflage with environment. He has not neglected to disguise his Beretta 70/90 rifle either.

One thing we had to consider when we picked snipers was how they would react to shooting a target they could quite clearly see was a human being, and not just a grey blur that is already threatening the firer. We looked for a degree of 'compartmentalization' in our snipers. He might see someone shaving, standing in a meal queue,

see someone shaving, standing in a meal queue, or whatever, but he had to see them as the enemy. As far as we could, in training we used targets that were not obviously military or threatening.

That in practice went as far as making the targets look like women and children.

To a comfortable civilian in a comfortable arm-chair such techniques may seem grotesque. Nonetheless, snipers are supposed to be emotion-less killers, and training has to prepare them for the consequences of their actions. As Canadian Major J.R. Bagnall has said, snipers 'will be exposed to mental and physical stress above the normal in com-bat. Psychological make-up is paramount. A sniper must have the self-confidence that enables him to kill when the time comes. At the same time he must have a conscience that keeps him from killing just for the sake of killing; ... [he] must be prepared to stalk and kill in a more personal way than is the case in most combat situations.' And he added, pertinent-ly: 'Snipers should always be volunteers.'

Sniper training is designed to stretch men to their limits, and teach them that they can endure the apparently impossible and the definitely appalling. Some courses are deliberately structured to be more taxing than anything they are likely to meet in real life. But only the battlefield will show whether even

L85A1 (SA80 Individual Weapon)

Country of origin	United Kingdom
Calibre	5.56 x 45mm (.219 x 1.78 inches)
Overall length	78.7cm (31 inches)
Barrel length	51.8cm (20.4 inches)
Weight	4.5kg (10lb)

• Butt-pad on rear of receiver; synthetic pistol grip and fore-end
• Infantry models with 4x optical SUSAT sights; support-troop models with a front blade and rear peep
• Gas-operated, self-loading, selective
• Detachable 30-round box magazine

This rifle, like the Martini Henry 100 years before it, remains the subject of controversy about its effectiveness. Like the Martini Henry, it was produced to a timetable and a budget, and like the Martini Henry, it seems destined to be replaced when political pride can be compromised enough to prevent further jeopardy to British troops.

The weapon is mentioned here because trainee British snipers complete the basic course with this weapon; which is less than useful because the ammunition is generic to the longer-bar-relled section-support weapons, so there is a tell-tale muzzle flash from the SA80 when fired. Adolf Hitler commented on this problem in the 1930s, so one assumes that the lessons he learned in the 1914–18 war have been lost on current British Government arms buyers.

Measure for measure

There are several methods a sniper can use to estimate the distances between himself and the various features of the landscape he's watching. By knowing these, he can quickly work out the range to a specific target passing through that area.

• The paper-strip method is useful to determine distances of over 1000m (1100 yards). It calls for a large-scale map (or an aerial photograph of known scale) that includes the target area and the sniper team's position, and it calls for skilled map-reading. The sniper puts the edge of a long strip of paper on the map and makes a mark on the paper at the team position and another at the location of the feature or position he's interested in. He puts the paper against the map's bar scale (usually printed at the bottom of the map), and aligns one of his marks with the zero on the scale. Then he reads the distance on the scale between the two marks.

• The 100-yard (92m) unit-of-measure method calls for the sniper to be able to visualise a distance of 100 yards on the ground. For ranges up to 500 yards (457m), the sniper reckons how many 100-yard increments there are between his position and his objective. Beyond 500 yards, he estimates the point halfway to the objective and determines the number of 100-yard increments to the halfway point, then doubles it to find how far away the objective is.

• The appearance-of-object method is used to determine range by judging and analysing the apparent size and the visible details of a distant object. For this method to work with any degree of accuracy, the sniper must be familiar with the way characteristic details of the objects appear at various ranges – a matter of practice and experience.

• Using the bracketing method, the sniper assumes that the target is no more than X distance but no less than Y distance away. The mid-point between X and Y will be the estimate of the distance to the target. This method is best used to back up, or should be confirmed by, other estimates of distance.

• The sniper team can also use a range card to determine ranges throughout the target area. Once a target is seen, the team determines where it is located on the card and then reads the proper range to the target. The range card will, of course, have been previously, and painstakingly, drawn beforehand, using a combination of maps, photographs and other ways of estimating the range to various features of the terrain the sniper is observing.

• On the battlefield, conditions are rarely ideal for the sniper. A single technique for estimating range may not give any tolerable certainty of the distances between various features of the terrain, or the target, and the sniper's position. For example, terrain with a lot of dead space (blind areas created by the rise and fall of the ground, or the sniper's position in the upper storeys of a building) restricts the usefulness of the 100-yard method. Likewise, the appearance-of-object method is instantly limited by poor visibility. But applying two or more of the above techniques to work out an unknown range should give a useful approximation of the true distance.

• Some telescopic sights have 'mil dots' etched on to the thin crosshairs of the reticle. A mil is 1/6400th of a circle, and the dots on the reticle are one mil apart, centre to centre. An object a third of a metre square (3 feet square) fills that space if it's 915m (1000 yards) away. At 823m (900 yards) an object taking up a mil space on the reticle is 81cm (32 inches) wide, and at 731m (800 yards) it will be 73.5cm (29 inches) wide – and so on down to 30.5cm (12 inches) at 274m (300 yards), 17.8cm (7 inches) at 183m (200 yards), and 10cm (4 inches) at 91.5m (100 yards). Using mil dots successfully means already knowing how wide or tall the object or the part of it that you're looking at is (a matter of experience and some learning), then back-calculating to find the range.

• If a sniper has (or can scrounge) laser range-finding kit, he should use it, because these gizmos – which today are highly portable – can show the range to a target with extreme accuracy. The sniper should aim and support the laser gun in much the same way as he aims his rifle, in order to provide the most accurate reading he can. If the target is particularly small or distant, aiming the laser at a larger object nearby (such as a building, vehicle, tree or prominent rock), or at one that's at the same distance from the sniper, will give a sufficiently accurate indication of the range.

CHAPTER 4

TEN-FOUR BLUE

The world of the police sniper

'A sniper should be the type that attempts to fix something that isn't broken, just to see if an even better technique can be developed'
— Richard Fairburn

Those who know are emphatic that a police sniper's job is different from that of a military sniper. Many of the same talents may be required of the police sniper as are needed by the military, and all snipers need to be masters of marksmanship, fieldcraft and tactics. It is how they apply those skills, and the circumstances in which they operate, that makes the difference.

Two differences stand out above all others. The first is that a police sniper rarely operates on his own: he is almost always part of a larger team — and bearing on that is his different status in law from a military sniper. The second is that the police sniper tends to be much closer to his targets than a military sniper. Not for him the brilliant 1000-yard shot. At the same time, the demands on his skill as a marksman are paradoxically that much higher. He cannot afford to miss, because the lives of others — such as hostages, or his fellow officers — are very likely at stake.

A CHOICE OF TARGETS

To put the issue very simply, under the international laws of warfare, a military sniper, like any other

Left: Police sniping has many of its own peculiarities, such as the need to shoot through glass in an urban environment.

127

Above: A Peruvian Army sniper keeps watch over the Japanese embassy compound during the long siege that began in December 1996 and ended after a four month stand-off.

combatant, can shoot whom he likes as long as his target is identifiable as an enemy. He does not need to feel that he or anyone else is in immediate danger from that enemy; it's enough that the target is on the other side. That alone makes the prey a threat to the shooter's own forces. Generals of European armies may once have offered their opposite numbers the chance to take the first shot, but modern rules of engagement don't call for combat units or snipers to give any warning of an attack. If this were the convention, the ambush, the Claymore, and the whole concept of 'the element of surprise' would have to be ditched as legitimate means of waging war, let alone the farce that sniping would become.

Things are not quite as simple for the police sniper. In his book *Police Rifles*, Richard Fairburn gives the three broad guidelines that in most jurisdictions govern the use of deadly force by the police:

1. A police officer has the right to use deadly force in defense of his/her own life. They may defend against any force directed against them that is likely to cause death or great bodily harm.
2. A police officer has the right to use deadly force in defense of another human life. Again, this relates to force or the threat of force likely to cause death or great bodily harm to another.
3. A police officer may use deadly force to prevent the escape of a dangerous felon that has used or threatened force during the commission of his crime, has the means to inflict harm, and is still

in possession of the potential force during his/her escape. Most jurisdictions further restrict this use of force to the degree that an escaping felon is unlikely to be taken into custody by a lesser means of force and that the felon will further endanger society if allowed to escape.

Fairburn adds: 'The law does not allow police officers to act as judge, jury, or executioner, and many wrongful death lawsuits are based upon this premise.'

It is clear enough, however, that in most circumstances in which the police sniper has to shoot, he will be depending on a rational interpretation of the third point – just as much as on his own accurate interpretation of the situation as it develops – to justify his shot. Fairburn comments: 'If hostages are being held, if innocents or officers have already been harmed, or if the felon is clearly unwilling to surrender without the likelihood of injuries or death, latitude may be granted to use deadly force to terminate the incident.' This adequately covers eventualities such as assassinations, armed sieges and robberies in which the villains have already used extreme violence.

To illustrate the demands made on the police sniper, one might take as example a robbery gone awry in which the villains, in the hope of making a getaway without being apprehended, have taken hostages. The police team responding to this emergency will have at least one sniper on hand.

Below: This staged hostage scenario gives an idea of the type of target faced by police snipers. Unlike the military sniper, the police marksman must hit and disable the right person with his first shot, while being aware of the subsequent path of his bullet.

Assuming that the sniper is able to see the perpetrators, he should be able to distinguish them from the hostages and other innocent bystanders. As like as not, the hostages will be used as human shields, leaving as little of any bad guy exposed as possible. If (for whatever reason) it falls to the sniper to eliminate the threat, he has to judge his shot very precisely. Not only is he unlikely to get another chance to shoot – a miss will very probably bring a lethal reaction from the bad guys, and one or more hostages may die. That in itself could well result in the sniper being sued for contributing to those deaths. If he shoots, misses the villain and kills the hostage because of misjudging the moment, he's virtually certain to be sued. In Britain, he might even be prosecuted for murder or at least manslaughter.

In similar circumstances – such as embassy sieges, or skyjackings, which tend to be handled by special forces teams – military snipers are not liable in this way. And the military sniper, if he has his fieldcraft and his tactics right, can afford to wait for his targets to expose themselves just nicely. When hoping to hit a very high-value and rarely seen target such as an enemy general, the military sniper has to do the best he can and perhaps take a chancy shot. If he misses but knocks out a staff officer of field rank he may still have done the state some service. Likewise, he can afford to take shots that are less than a sure hit: some of them will reach their target, and those that don't will still contribute to the psychological damage the sniper can inflict on an enemy unit as a whole. And hardly ever does he have to worry about imperfectly placed bullets killing friendly forces or innocent bystanders.

In contrast, the police sniper cannot afford to miss, ever. Someone else's life besides the target's is almost certainly in his hands. At the very least, the criminal may escape. And the military sniper is not working against the clock, as a police officer almost always is. Despite notable exceptions (such as the fiasco at Waco, Texas, in 1993), deadly force will generally be brought to bear by law-enforcement officers only when all other means of resolving the emergency have failed. And this means that by the time the sniper is called on to shoot, negotiations have broken down, the bad guys are at the end of their tether, and matters are becoming unpredictable.

JUDGEMENT CALL

It is a curiosity of the international conventions of war that a soldier, sniper or not, cannot use hollow-pointed or soft-pointed ammunition. But the police sniper can. The risk that his bullet will pass through his target to strike an innocent victim is thus reduced considerably. A hollowpoint will tend to fragment, causing more damage to the target, while remaining in the body. This is one advantage the police sniper has. But all the other factors add to the pressure on the police sniper. They may affect his judgement, and may end up being debated less than sympathetically in court. 'The police sniper,' writes John L. Plaster, a recognised authority, 'must keep in mind that his every move must be justifiable, and that he especially will have to "articulate" the threat he perceived to legitimize his shot.'

Plaster has a simple but far-reaching rule of thumb to call on in making such a judgement:

a police sniper's authority to fire need not require an order from an on-scene supervisor. It should be generated by the situation itself. Ask yourself, 'If I had a pistol and I was 10 feet from the suspect, can I justify using deadly force?' Should the answer be, 'Yes,' your only distinction as a sniper is the distance, not the justification.

Plaster emphasises too an important and related distinction between police and military snipers, which is that

a police sniper ... must have the capacity to say 'NO!'

He must have the guts to assess the situation honestly, weigh this against his rifle and his own

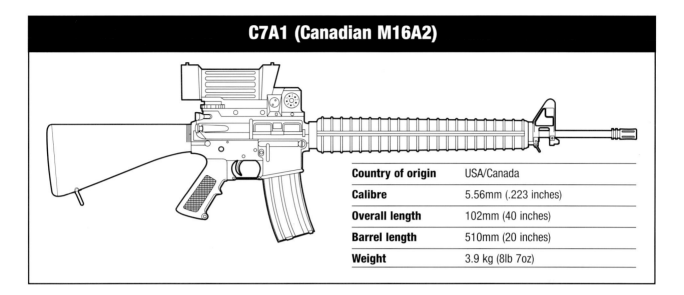

C7A1 (Canadian M16A2)

Country of origin	USA/Canada
Calibre	5.56mm (.223 inches)
Overall length	102mm (40 inches)
Barrel length	510mm (20 inches)
Weight	3.9 kg (8lb 7oz)

abilities, and let his supervisor know if the shot can be taken. Often leaders do not fully appreciate a rifleman's capabilities; passively accommodating their desires can lead to disaster.

The matter of distance is also, as noted, a crucial distinction between the military and the police sniper.

Rarely, if ever, is a police sniper surrounded by heavily armed hostiles itching to locate and wipe him out. Almost equally rarely – most crimes occur where there are most people, which is in cities – is it difficult for a police sniper to get into a firing position that's significantly distant from his quarry. His rifle is typically zeroed at 90m (100 yards); he should be able to get at least that close to the target and, indeed, usually does. FBI statistics show that in the USA police snipers are, on average, a mere 64.5m (71 yards) from their targets.

The military sniper prefers to keep his target at a safe distance – safe, that is, for the sniper. Most modern combat rifles are not very accurate beyond about 360m (400 yards), and then only in cool, skilled hands. So a military sniper will stay out of range of the weapons that the majority of his opponents (enemy snipers excepted) will be carrying,

knowing full well that his own kit will be thoroughly effective at twice that distance.

Because of the reduced ranges over which police snipers commonly operate, scoped versions of combat rifles are often used. The Ottawa, Canada, Tactical Group for example use 5.56mm C7A1 (M16A2) assault rifles for medium-range targets alongside .308 Remingtons. Miami's Metro-Dade Special Response Team use the CAR-15 (civilian M16) backed up by Remington M24s for longer-range work. Israel's Ya'sa'm (Special Patrol Unit), whilst not strictly snipers, also favour the CAR-15 with scope for use in the crowded, narrow streets of Jerusalem.

The police sniper rarely has to face the problems of a long stalk and withdrawal, but similar risks, along with the possibility of reasonably effective counter-sniper fire, can certainly arise in circumstances such as sieges against members of radical political groups holed up in some isolated farm, or when dealing with large-scale drug trafficking operations, which may well occur in secluded, and possibly guarded, areas. But the police sniper usually has the advantages of a range within the zero of his rifle, little or no chance of retaliatory fire, and no need to exfiltrate himself from his firing position

undetected. But that ascendancy brings with it a corresponding need to make the solitary chance he will have for a shot a decisive one.

Directly bearing on the police sniper's paramount need to maintain an unbroken record of 'one shot, one kill' is his rifle. Some police departments maintain more snipers than they do sniping rifles, but while they save some money on hardware they do their marksmen no favours. Every shooter is idiosyncratic to some extent, and one man's zero for a given rifle may be quite distinct from another's. A police sniper may have to go to work at a moment's notice, and if he has to share a rifle he cannot be sure that its current zero is his own. That uncertainty will not only add to the stress he inevitably faces on an operation, but any liability for a misplaced shot could be considerably more damaging for the department than for him. However, when a man has a rifle that for all intents and purposes he can regard as his own, he can do more than rely on it when on call. He can practice with it regularly and often, whenever and wherever is practicable, and master both it and his art. Then, when he is needed, he can have absolute confidence in himself as well as his weapon.

CHANGE AS GOOD AS REST

When it comes to actual operations, further distinctions between military and police sniping work become apparent. The military sniper sets out with a distinct plan in mind, one that may have involved weeks of preparation and rehearsal. He works in constant personal danger, both because he is operating behind enemy lines (or very close to them), or because when he is not, his effect – both materially and psychologically – on the enemy is so powerful that he himself becomes a high-priority target. Concealment, care and cunning are his greatest aids in either circumstance.

Left: Italian police snipers practise shooting from a rooftop position, using a Mauser SR86 and an H&K MSG90. In a real call-out, multiple snipers would be dispersed to give maximum coverage.

Above: This Italian NOCS anti-terrorist police sniper remains unobtrusive in an urban environment. He is well supported on a table, back in the shadows of a room and his Mauser 86SR is camouflaged to reduce glint and break up its outline.

But he is also helped by his need to be always on the move, if often at less than a snail's pace. If he is any good, he will be hidden somewhere else entirely by the time anyone discovers where his last lethal shot came from, if they find out at all. The military sniper's constant movement also keeps his mind unfailingly on the alert, for he is always on the lookout for new targets and always preoccupied by the demand to remain invisible, day or night.

This is exhausting work. John Plaster says:

The military sniper's stresses eventually reduce him to being combat ineffective. Having run many operations deep behind enemy lines, I can tell firsthand that such 24-hour dangers will wear you down in about four or five days. In SOG [Study & Observation Group – a clandestine special forces unit operating in Viet Nam] we were deadly effective at sneaking and hiding and even outmaneuvering bloodhounds and specially trained trackers, but only for less than a week.

The police sniper's job, however, is almost the exact opposite of this, and wise commanders will always be sure to make allowances and organise shifts accordingly.

The law-enforcement rifleman does not have the luxury of knowing when or where he will be called to go into action, or of preplanning it. A major emergency, requiring his services, can happen at any time. In addition to the stress involved in any particular operation, the police sniper has to live every hour of his everyday life in the shadow of that extra tension. As John Plaster puts it, 'He could be having lunch with his fiancee one minute and 10 minutes later have a mass-murderer in his crosshairs.'

The police sniper doesn't pick his targets: in effect, they pick him. He doesn't have to crawl through mud or sand, attacked by insects, always in rational fear of an enemy who's only too keen to kill him. He swaps that species of mental and physical strain for the tedium of having to watch a few targets – and maybe only one – for hours at a time, while all the time remaining sufficiently mentally alert to judge whether or not to shoot.

A military sniper can remain focused on his job for four or five days but, paradoxically, his awareness of the danger all around him, his ability to move, and his change (and choice) of targets help to provide the stimulus that fuels and motivates him throughout that gruelling time. Staring at the same scene through the scope of a rifle, having to be alert to the slightest change in the details of what's happening, can soon take on all the exhilarating aspects of watching paint dry – but that's what a police sniper has to do, as well as maintain the mental and physical edge required for a one-stop shot.

Experience suggests that few people can sustain this level of concentration for much more than half a day. Police commanders who appreciate the implications of that fact will have their snipers work only short shifts with their finger on the trigger, ensuring that they stay as fresh and alert as is practically possible. That requirement becomes particularly apparent when one considers that most incidents that have turned on the presence and proficiency of a police sniper either have been resolved within an hour or two, or have dragged out over a day or two. It's when an operation doesn't conclude swiftly that police snipers need to treat their need for rest breaks and sleep as seriously as they hone their skill at arms.

ON THE JOB

So far, and in passing, we've touched on only a few of the tasks that come a police sniper's way. Because of his expertise with a rifle, it's easy enough to think of the sniper as purely a specialist shooter. It's also obvious, however, that snipers in all forms of uniformed service actually spend very little time shooting when on an operation, but an awful lot of hours waiting and watching. It became apparent very early in the history of sniping that the hidden vantage points, long hours, and meticulous observation that the work entailed, could be put to good use by others besides the sniper himself. The sniper is a supremely valuable intelligence-gatherer, and on policing operations observation makes up the bulk of his work.

Snipers will be deployed in the 'classic' hostage/siege incident already mentioned. Even before SWAT or Special Operations units arrive, against the possibility that they may have to take the besieged premises by storm, a sniper may well be in place to back up (most probably unarmed) negotiators and keep them informed of what is happening inside the building. They will also back up more straightforward raids by tactical units on objectives like crack houses, or when taking high-level criminals into custody, or when dealing with the siege or entry of terrorist 'safe houses'. Here again they will be in position to support their colleagues with precision fire, but equally to give them, by radio, a picture of the targets, their movements and their immediate environment that officers on the ground may not be able to see. Says Richard Fairburn:

> While a sniper must be a master shooter, his primary mission for [his] team will be as the gatherer of intelligence. A sniper must be trained

Above: An urban environment affords terrorists almost limitless hiding places, but just as many potential sniping positions for the police and Special Forces. This view of a Parisian tower block was seen during preparations for the 1998 World Cup.

to see and remember small details. These details must then be reported without any embellishment or interpretation. The team commander will be sorting through many items of intelligence, and the sniper's eye-witness information must be the most accurate he has. Just as a sniper does not generally make the decision to use deadly force, he must neither make determinations based solely on the intelligence data he collects and reports. To those in the know, a first-class sniper is the single most valuable element a response team can field. In fact, snipers and negotiators can often contain and control a situation long enough for a

REMINGTON 700

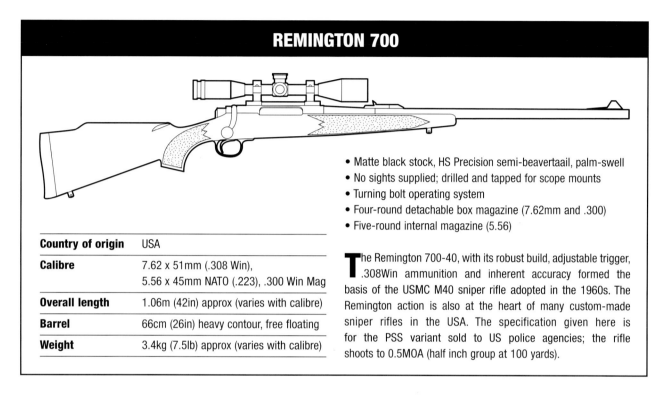

- Matte black stock, HS Precision semi-beavertaail, palm-swell
- No sights supplied; drilled and tapped for scope mounts
- Turning bolt operating system
- Four-round detachable box magazine (7.62mm and .300)
- Five-round internal magazine (5.56)

Country of origin	USA
Calibre	7.62 x 51mm (.308 Win), 5.56 x 45mm NATO (.223), .300 Win Mag
Overall length	1.06m (42in) approx (varies with calibre)
Barrel	66cm (26in) heavy contour, free floating
Weight	3.4kg (7.5lb) approx (varies with calibre)

The Remington 700-40, with its robust build, adjustable trigger, .308Win ammunition and inherent accuracy formed the basis of the USMC M40 sniper rifle adopted in the 1960s. The Remington action is also at the heart of many custom-made sniper rifles in the USA. The specification given here is for the PSS variant sold to US police agencies; the rifle shoots to 0.5MOA (half inch group at 100 yards).

fully trained assault team to arrive at a remote location.

The sniper provides long-range intelligence and support too in undercover and security operations.

Drug stings often call for undercover policemen to make ostensible deals with traffickers, and the officers directly involved will frequently work unarmed. The sniper is there to protect them should the need arise and to observe the wider picture, and can corroborate evidence gathered by those directly on the scene. On ceremonial occasions, snipers placed strategically on or in buildings on a parade route act in practice more as observers than as shooters – giving colleagues on the ground information about crowd movements, traffic and signs of suspicious activity or individuals. Most of these can be handled swiftly and easily by officers on the ground, but the ability to keep a suspect in the crosshairs – both before and after they arrive – both reduces any potential risk

and maintains a flow of vital information to those responding.

The same advantages of 'high cover', and the same calls on the sniper's talents, come into play in most operations involving security for VIPs. In the vast majority of such operations, no threat emerges – so the major part of a sniper's job remains observation and reporting. The set task may consist of no more than surveillance when reconnoitring suspected drug factories, remote airfields, warehouses or other infrastructure of the criminal fraternity. In these cases the sniper may carry only basic personal defence weapons, but otherwise will come nearest to the work of his military counterpart, since he will have to infiltrate the area, and return to whatever rendezvous has been arranged, without being detected. Then he will need to know, and apply, all the arts of camouflage and concealment – and possibly escape and evasion – routinely used by the military. These may not make up a large proportion of the police sniper's work in some areas, but he will

VAIME SSR Mk1 Sniper Rifle

Country of origin	Finland
Calibre	7.62 x 51mm (.3 x 2 inches)
Overall length	1.18m (46 1/2 inches)
Weight	4.1kg (9lb)

- Barrel fully shrouded with sound suppressor
- Nonreflective plastic stock, with bipod
- Any optical/night vision system can be fitted using adaptors; no iron sights fitted
- Turning-bolt operating system
- Detachable five-round box magazine

The Vaime SSR Mk1 is used by Britain's SAS and other special forces. The integral suppressor makes for a much shorter and more manoeuvrable weapon, and a quieter one, than a rifle with a silencer fitted as a barrel extension.

need to know them should the need arise, and have the appropriate kit ready for use.

This kit not only includes a choice of snipers' rifles for medium and long-range shooting, but appropriate optics for day and night use. The Portland, Oregon, police's Emergency Support Unit (ESU) are equipped with the Remington 700 .308 rifle, much favoured by police forces and also used as the basis for many of the FBI and Secret Service's custom-built sniper weapons. To this basic weapon, the Portland ESU fit a Leupold Ultra M3 3.5 x 10 sniper scope for daytime use and a starlight-amplifying Litton Starscope for night-time observation and engagement.

One rifle designed from the outset for counter-terrorist (CT) use is the Finnish Vaime Mk 2. This silenced, 7.62-mm weapon is one of several types used by the US Secret Service's counter-sniping teams, and in its Mk 1 SSR form, by Britain's SAS. The integral silencer reduces its effective range to about 200m (218 yards), however. Also from Finland, home of many great sniping rifles over the

years, are the Sako TRG-21 and -41, the latter chambered for the .338 Lapua Magnum cartridge for improved accuracy over longer ranges.

INSTANT EFFECT

Nonetheless, despite the time and effort invested in observation, the police sniper may have to take the decisive shot. While all incidents will call for a sure-fire hit, positively incapacitating the target will be sufficient in many. The one occasion when an instant kill is absolutely necessary occurs when a hostage is being held at gunpoint. In that case the shot not only has to be lethal – it has to drop the perpetrator before he has a chance to react, even through an involuntary reflex action to being hit, and kill the hostage. There is a way to prevent even reflex action – and that is to sever all the neurological connections between the brain and the muscles.

This can be done – by putting a bullet through the medulla oblongata, or 'brain stem', which links the brain itself to the spinal cord. Through it pass all the nervous impulses (tiny electrical charges, in fact) from the brain to the body. Cutting it should prevent both the feared conscious reaction by the target – killing the hostage – or a convulsive reflex response that has the same result. A hit in the spine above the shoulder blades, or into the neural motor strips that run just above the ears, will have the same effect. Which is all very well, but these are extremely small targets. The neural motor strips are about 25mm (one inch) wide. The spine and the brain stem are both about 37mm (1.5 inches) across. To hit any of them within 90m (100 yards) or less, the sniper will have to make a perfect shot. This is hard enough. Beyond that distance, even the finest marksman with the most accurate sniper rifle would be depending as much on luck as judgement in making the attempt. And that, in any case, calls for the target to be at just the right angle to the shooter. To hit the brain stem, the bullet has to strike the target between the nose and teeth, full-face to the shooter, or strike the base of the skull when the target has the back of his head square to the shooter.

Sako TRG-21/41 Sniper Rifle

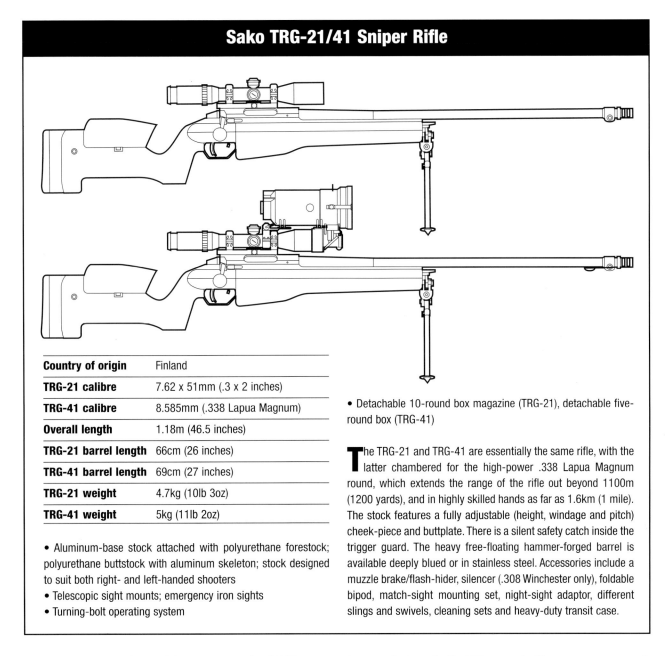

Country of origin	Finland
TRG-21 calibre	7.62 x 51mm (.3 x 2 inches)
TRG-41 calibre	8.585mm (.338 Lapua Magnum)
Overall length	1.18m (46.5 inches)
TRG-21 barrel length	66cm (26 inches)
TRG-41 barrel length	69cm (27 inches)
TRG-21 weight	4.7kg (10lb 3oz)
TRG-41 weight	5kg (11lb 2oz)

• Aluminum-base stock attached with polyurethane forestock; polyurethane buttstock with aluminum skeleton; stock designed to suit both right- and left-handed shooters
• Telescopic sight mounts; emergency iron sights
• Turning-bolt operating system

• Detachable 10-round box magazine (TRG-21), detachable five-round box (TRG-41)

The TRG-21 and TRG-41 are essentially the same rifle, with the latter chambered for the high-power .338 Lapua Magnum round, which extends the range of the rifle out beyond 1100m (1200 yards), and in highly skilled hands as far as 1.6km (1 mile). The stock features a fully adjustable (height, windage and pitch) cheek-piece and buttplate. There is a silent safety catch inside the trigger guard. The heavy free-floating hammer-forged barrel is available deeply blued or in stainless steel. Accessories include a muzzle brake/flash-hider, silencer (.308 Winchester only), foldable bipod, match-sight mounting set, night-sight adaptor, different slings and swivels, cleaning sets and heavy-duty transit case.

However, Martin Feckler MD, a retired US army surgeon, has good news for snipers and bad news for those who take hostages at gunpoint. Feckler points out that the medulla oblongata is the point of least resistance between the brain and the spinal cord; everywhere else inside the brain is armoured by the bone of the skull. When a bullet penetrates soft material like flesh or the brain, it creates a temporary, massive cavity in its wake. This in turn creates huge pressure on the material, and can destroy its ability to function – hence the devastating effect of a so-called 'gut shot'. A bullet entering the brain behaves in exactly the same way, except that (unlike in the rest of the body) the pressure of the cavitation effect is contained by the skull. That pressure has to go somewhere, and it takes the line of least resistance, venting through the brain stem. While bone and bullet fragments destroy the brain, the brain stem is torn apart by the secondary effects of the hit.

Feckler considers that any effective shot to the brain will suffice; one to the lower half of the brain will certainly, and automatically, produce the required effect. This creates a target area – or margin of error – for the sniper of about the size of a fist, which is at least four times larger than demanded for the perfect shot. And the shot can be taken from almost any angle. Richard Fairburn puts the advantage in a real-life context:

Below: Public appearances by VIPs can be a security nightmare, and these photographers are getting too close to the French president's car. Part of the police sniper's job is to occupy potential terrorist shooting positions.

Dr Fackler's concern is that a police sniper can make an error in judgment caused by the pin-point accuracy required to hit the brain stem. Fackler relates an incident in which a police officer was being held hostage. The police sniper avoided a brain stem shot, feeling it too difficult under the circumstances. Instead of taking a head shot, the sniper placed a .223-caliber bullet in the felon's chest and the hostage/officer died because the felon was not stopped instantly. If the police sniper had been trained that any brain shot would produce the desired results, the hostage/officer would probably be alive today.

This event also demonstrates the virtue of using a heavier calibre than the lightweight .223-inch round for sniping. A chest shot from a .308 (7.62mm) Winchester NATO round would have caused far more damage, and may well have incapacitated the perpetrator sufficiently to save the hostage's life.

Above: The most powerful rifle in use with police and anti-terrorist units is the .50-calibre Barrett M82A1, seen here in the hands of an Italian Groupe Interventional Speciale sniper. It can disable a vehicle or aircraft at a range of over 2000m (6562 ft).

Fairburn also draws attention to a further key point, namely

that the body is more likely to relax from a shot, not tense. Most neurological experts agree that a sudden shock to the central nervous system will result in the muscles going slack, not convulsively pulling a trigger. This means we have been training to make an unnecessarily difficult shot, a shot we don't need to make.

Among the more popular .300 and .308-calibre weapons for police and counter-terrorist use are the Remington 700/40 and the SIG-Sauer SSG-2000/3000 series. The latter is more popular outside

Above: French RAID commandos practise clearing a Eurostar train. The sniper at right covers his comrades from adversaries who might appear from the next carriage. 'Tubular assaults' (trains, planes, buses) are amongst the hardest of police operations.

the USA and is available in a variety of calibres for different uses. Units such as Argentina's Seccion Fuerzas Especiales (a branch of the National Gendarmerie) prefer the .308 SSG-2000 with Schmidt & Bender sniping scopes for use in their field of jurisdiction; the countryside, towns and airports outside the capital and its hinterland. Such work often involves operating against isolated terrorist camps or drug factories at ranges greater than those usually regarded as normal for police work.

THROUGH GLASS DARKLY

The other problematic shot for the police sniper is the one that has to be taken through glass. Frangible as it is, glass still acts to deflect a bullet from its path when struck at an angle, and absorbs a fair proportion of a bullet's energy even when hit

square on. Knowing how to deal with this problem is vital for police officers, since most sieges involve buildings with windows, and the sniper will be looking through them to observe what he can of what's happening inside. And that means he may have to shoot through them.

Here again the calibre of the sniper's weapon becomes crucial. The view of most experts, but by no means all police procurement officers, is that the 7.62mm (.308-inch) round and on occasion the very powerful .300-inch Winchester Magnum round are the most useful for sniping. The effects of glass on a bullet's behaviour bear this view out. The .223-inch

SIG-Sauer SSG2000

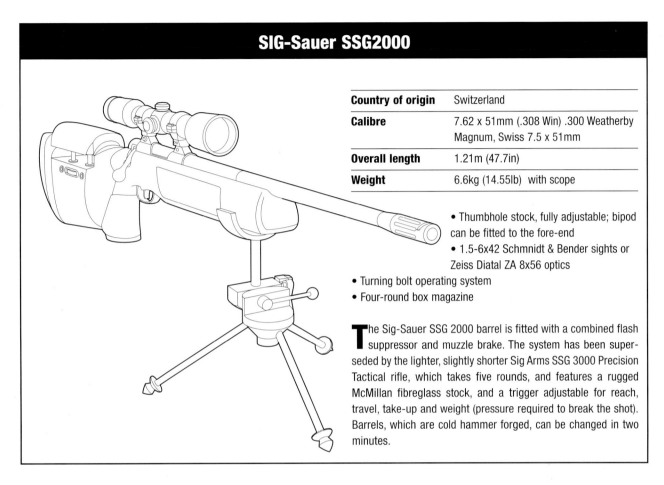

Country of origin	Switzerland
Calibre	7.62 x 51mm (.308 Win) .300 Weatherby Magnum, Swiss 7.5 x 51mm
Overall length	1.21m (47.7in)
Weight	6.6kg (14.55lb) with scope

• Thumbhole stock, fully adjustable; bipod can be fitted to the fore-end
• 1.5-6x42 Schmnidt & Bender sights or Zeiss Diatal ZA 8x56 optics
• Turning bolt operating system
• Four-round box magazine

The Sig-Sauer SSG 2000 barrel is fitted with a combined flash suppressor and muzzle brake. The system has been superseded by the lighter, slightly shorter Sig Arms SSG 3000 Precision Tactical rifle, which takes five rounds, and features a rugged McMillan fibreglass stock, and a trigger adjustable for reach, travel, take-up and weight (pressure required to break the shot). Barrels, which are cold hammer forged, can be changed in two minutes.

SIG-Sauer SSG2000

Kinetic energy in joules (and ft/lb)

	At the muzzle	At 182m (200 yards)	At 363m (400 yards)	At 545m (600 yards)
.223	1871 (1380)	1254 (925)	644 (475)	509 (375)
.308	3417 (2520)	2536 (1870)	1837 (1355)	1315 (970)

Velocity in m/sec (and ft/sec)

	At the muzzle	At 182m (200 yards)	At 363m (400 yards)	At 545m (600 yards)
.223	915 (3000)	750 (2460)	604 (1980)	475 (1560)
.308	792 (2600)	683 (2240)	582 (1910)	491 (1610)

Right: Airports may need the services of a sniper as part of their security team. Local anti-terrorist teams often train at the airport on a regular basis. This sniper with an H&K G-3SG1 is part of Milan Linate's own territorial Caribinieri unit.

round still favoured by some police departments for sniping usually fragments on hitting glass at any angle. What's left of the bullet may not be large enough, or retain enough energy, to make a significant hit. Comparing the .223's velocity and kinetic energy with the .308's at several ranges gives an unmistakable picture of the .308's superiority. Statistics are for Federal Match ammunition in both calibres (see table on p143).

The .308 starts slower, but retains speed over distance, so that at 545m (600 yards) (an extreme distance for a police sniper) it's actually travelling faster than the lighter .223, and it retains this edge out to beyond 910m (1000 yards). The kinetic energy figures are even more graphic. At the muzzle the .308 is carrying 82 per cent more energy than the .223, more than twice as much at 182m (200 yards), and nearly 2.6 times as much at 545m (600 yards). Plainly the .308 will fly truer through glass, even at an angle, than the .223. Using full-metal-jacket (FMJ) or 'military hardball' ammunition also reduces the bullet's tendency to fragment. Hollowpoint bullets are certainly more effective on an unimpeded target, as they flatten and release all or most of their energy into the body, but they naturally become unpredictable on hitting a medium like glass, which will itself make them deform.

Experiments by the US Marine Corps and others have revealed some curious facts about the way bullets and glass behave on contact. The glass tends to shatter in a cone – the smallest fragments nearest to the point of impact, and the largest furthest away – but mostly at right angles to its surfaces, no matter at what angle the bullet itself strikes. Snipers will have to take this into account when weighing up the chances of any bystanders or hostages being wounded by flying glass, and balancing the risks entailed in their shot.

Right: Airports may need the services of a sniper as part of their security team. Local anti-terrorist teams often train at the airport on a regular basis. This sniper with an H&K G-3SG1 is part of Milan Linate's own territorial Caribinieri unit.

As for the bullet, it tends to curve inward slightly, into the angle at which it strikes the glass. The theory is (in John Plaster's words) that 'one edge of the bullet touches first, which probably causes friction and pulls the projectile slightly inward.' With FMJ bullets, the copper jacket is torn away on impact, but its lead core largely retains its integrity and ploughs on regardless in much the same direction as before. The angular deflection is usually small enough not

to affect the lethality of the shot within the ranges that police snipers operate, when the bullet retains much of its original velocity and energy.

The actual degree of deflection to be expected can of course be discovered by experimenting with as many varieties of glass as can be obtained. And, when called out to deal with an incident, the police sniper should try to find out as soon as possible what kind of glass he is facing. Then, he can adjust his aim to accommodate the behaviour of the bullet once it has broken the window. If for some reason he's working alone, he should try to set up his hide as near as possible at right angles to the glazing, to minimise the problem. The sure-fire answer to the imponderables presented by having to shoot through glass is to use two snipers. Both aim at the same target, and fire simultaneously. The very slight variations in performance between one round

Heckler & Koch G3

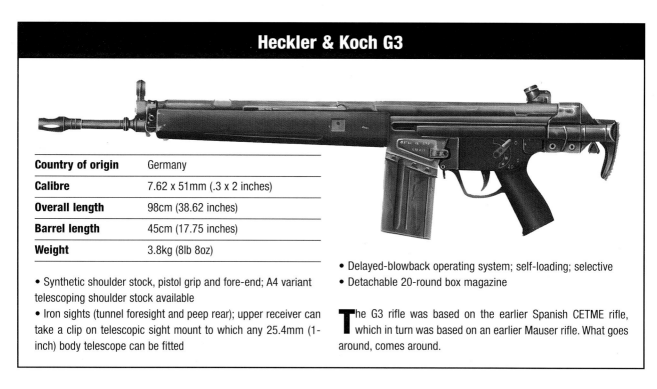

Country of origin	Germany
Calibre	7.62 x 51mm (.3 x 2 inches)
Overall length	98cm (38.62 inches)
Barrel length	45cm (17.75 inches)
Weight	3.8kg (8lb 8oz)

• Synthetic shoulder stock, pistol grip and fore-end; A4 variant telescoping shoulder stock available
• Iron sights (tunnel foresight and peep rear); upper receiver can take a clip on telescopic sight mount to which any 25.4mm (1-inch) body telescope can be fitted

• Delayed-blowback operating system; self-loading; selective
• Detachable 20-round box magazine

The G3 rifle was based on the earlier Spanish CETME rifle, which in turn was based on an earlier Mauser rifle. What goes around, comes around.

and another will ensure that one bullet will hit the glass first, shattering it, and leaving a clear field for the second bullet to reach the target a tiny fraction of a second later. Firing simultaneously also gives the target no appreciable time in which to react violently to the window bursting into pieces before the second bullet finds him.

The weapons used by police and counter-terrorist (CT) squads in the USA and elsewhere are many and varied. The Heckler & Koch company make a family of rifles that are widely used by police and military special forces teams. The two main rifles used for sniping are the H&K G3 heavy assault rifle and the PSG-1 sniper's rifle, both of which fire 7.62mm (.308) ammunition. The PSG-1 and its lighter, more streamlined development, the MSG90, are used by some forces, including Miami's, for CT work, as well as by the US Navy SEALS and Army Delta Force commandos for the same jobs. Some sub-machineguns such as the H&K MP5 can be used for precision shooting over short distances when the need arises. The MP5SD version is usu-

ally fitted with a scope and has the added benefit of being silenced, making it ideal for eliminating a terrorist watchman without alerting his colleagues.

FEELING THE NEED

In closing, we return to the theme with which we started this chapter: the differences between police and military snipers. One key difference, not mentioned earlier, is the social and psychological one. While historically the sniper has not been a popular figure on the battlefield – whichever side he's been on – the police sniper has been saddled with no such 'outsider' label. The reason is not difficult to grasp. Those he is prepared to shoot have already trampled on all civilised notions of acceptable – let alone 'fair', behaviour – by taking hostages, attempting an assassination, killing innocent people and so on. Depredations of the deranged first led to police in the USA being routinely armed with rifles. In Europe, terrorist activity by various left-wing revolutionary groups, and in the UK by the IRA and

Heckler & Koch PSG-1

- Roller-locked, delayed-blowback operating system
- Detachable 5- or 20-round box magazine

Country of origin	Germany
Calibre	7.62 x 51mm (.3 x 2 inches)
Overall length	1.2m (47.5 inches)
Barrel length	65cm (25.875 inches)
Weight including tripod	7.8kg (17lb 4oz)

- Stock in matte black high-impact plastic, adjustable for length; pivoting butt cap; vertically adjustable cheek-piece; target-type pistol grip with adjustable palm shelf
- Telescopic sight only: Hendsoldt 6 x 42, with reticle illumination; six settings from 100 to 600m (109–656 yards)

The PSG-1 is said by many to be the most accurate semi-automatic. PSG-1s are tested for 50 rounds of match ammunition into an 80mm (3.187-inch) bull at 300m (330 yards). Popular with special-ops and anti-terrorist units, the weapon is not as useful for military purposes. Since it ejects shells about 10m (10.9 yards), it can help an enemy identify the shooter's position, not just because the ejection attracts attention but also because, that far away, the brass shells are hard to collect and keep out of sight. Also, the PSG-1 can be fitted only with the Hensoldt 6 x 42 sight, set up with a range of only 600m (656 yards) – just the start of the optimal sniping range. It remains an outstanding police weapon, but is too expensive for most police agencies.

associated violent Irish nationalist factions, led to the formation of specialist units to handle their capture and to deal with a continuing rise in crime involving firearms.

American police were introduced to a new and deeply problematic threat to the civil peace in Western societies on 1 August 1966, when former US Marine Charles Whitman, a 25-year-old engineering student at the University of Texas at Austin, went on a deadly rampage from atop the 28-storey clock tower on his campus. Alwyn Barr, writing for the Texas State Historical Association, described what happened that day:

During the pre-dawn hours of August 1, 1966, Whitman killed his mother in her apartment and

his wife at their residence. Later in the morning he bought a variety of ammunition and a shotgun; about 11:30 a.m. he went to the university tower, taking with him a footlocker, six guns, knives, food, and water. After clubbing the receptionist (who later died) on the twenty-eighth floor about 11:45 a.m., he killed two persons and wounded two others who were coming up the stairs from the twenty-seventh floor. On the observation deck of the tower, at an elevation of 231 feet [70m], Whitman then opened fire on persons crossing the campus and on nearby streets, killing ten more people and wounding thirty-one more (one of whom died a week later). Police arrived and returned his fire, while other policemen worked their way into the tower. Several of the dead and wounded were moved to cover by students and other citizens while the firing continued. At 1:24 p.m. police and a deputized private citizen reached the observation deck, where police officers Ramiro Martinez and Houston McCoy shot and killed Whitman. Altogether, seventeen persons were killed, including Whitman, and thirty-one were wounded in one of the worst mass murders in modern United States history. An autopsy on Whitman's body revealed a brain tumor, but medical authorities disagreed over its effect on Whitman's actions.

Demonstrating all the fixated meticulousness of the psychopath, Whitman took with him up the tower: sandwiches, toilet paper, a transistor radio, a can of Spam, a jar of Planters Peanuts, canned fruit cocktail, a box of raisins, jerry cans containing water and petrol, rope, binoculars, canteens and a plastic bottle of Mennen spray deodorant. His six weapons were a 6mm Remington bolt-action rifle, a 7mm (.35-inch) Remington Model 700 Rifle, a Galesi-Brescia pistol, a .357 Magnum Smith & Wesson revolver, a .30-cal Garand M1 carbine, a 12-bore sawn-off shotgun, and over 700 rounds of ammunition.

Shortly after Whitman began shooting, more than 100 law officers from the Austin police, the Texas Rangers and even the local Secret Service office were on the scene. Whitman was killing and wounding people up to 910m (1000 yards) away, and was well concealed behind a waist-high balcony of brick and concrete columns. The police were armed only with rifles and shotguns, which were useless at that range. Citizens armed with deer rifles attempted a counterfire, but Whitman kept himself too well-hidden for them to be effective. His body count remains the highest for any mass murderer using a firearm.

Right: Police/anti-terrorist groups have replaced many of the hunting and ex-military rifles formerly used with sophisticated semi-automatics such as the Heckler & Koch PSG-1, which is perfect for the shorter distances over which police snipers work.

Above: The Steyr SSG69 can 'take out' a suspect without alerting his colleagues. A sound suppressor or silencer slows the bullet to subsonic speeds, reducing its range and hitting power.

Police departments took note, but often only so far as to arm one officer per shift with a rifle, and the choice of weapon was often idiosyncratic, as it was usually left up to the individual. Dedicated sniping and counter-sniper training seems to have been meagre to non-existent. Perhaps there was a feeling that such incidents were so rare that real investment against the chance of another was a waste of resources. After all, the golf-ball-sized tumour found in Whitman's brain was in the hypothalamus region, an area associated with, among other things, violent behaviour. In due course it turned out that Whitman had told the campus psychologist that he 'sometimes felt like going up to the tower and shooting people with a deer rifle'. Not unreasonably, the

psychologist regarded this as an empty threat: many students had made it before. No one seriously believed that such a peculiar set of circumstances would arise again.

Eight years later it became apparent that Whitman might represent something that, however unpredictable, would nonetheless become increasingly common in urban societies. In August 1974 ex-sailor Jimmy Essex, aged 23, went on a shooting spree at Howard Johnson's Motor Lodge in New Orleans. In the course of a full 11 hours, Essex killed seven people and wounded another 21 with a .44 Magnum Ruger carbine, holing himself up in the concrete cover of an elevator shaft on the hotel roof. Once more, law officers were outgunned. Essex was finally and comprehensively silenced by an M60 machine gun fired from a US Marine Corps helicopter.

Following that disaster, the concept of the police sniper, or 'counter-sniper', rapidly established itself and has been considerably refined – and mass killings involving firearms appear to be more common in most Western countries than once they were. Many incidents have been terminated when the perpetrator has turned a gun on himself. Few have actually lasted long enough for police to be able to intervene, either in a SWAT-style assault or through the subtler medium of a sniper. The tradecraft of the sniper, meanwhile, has proven invaluable in many other roles besides that of the counter-sniper, and is perhaps of more practical use in them than in its original concept. Having learned their value, police forces at least now actively seek out and train officers to be snipers.

Judging who, of serving police officers, will make a good sniper is not radically different from selecting sniper candidates in the military, except that, as noted, a police sniper's self-sufficiency doesn't have to extend as far as the soldier's. For the police sniper doesn't have to learn to accept that his colleagues will probably regard him in a slightly leery manner. Mental fortitude, physical toughness, high intelligence, patience and the hunting instinct are still vital.

Below: It is crucial that the rifle itself does not touch any hard surface. A beanbag, such as used by this Austrian GEK Anti-terrorism Unit sniper, has the advantage over a bipod of not having any harmonic resonance that can be passed to the rifle.

Above: The Elbit sniper co-ordination system, with a mini video camera linking the view from each rifle to the commander and other snipers.

In trying to make sniper selection a more exact discipline – and with one eye on liability suits as well, no doubt – police forces that can afford it have employed various psychological tests to weed out unsuitable candidates. One of the longest-established and best-respected among tests is the Minnesota Multi-Phasic Personality Inventory (MMPI). In the hands of a trained professional it can identify undesirable traits such as paranoia. However, is not as

good a predictor of future performance as another test, the Meyers-Briggs Personality Type Inventory.

In the Meyers-Briggs, each personality type is classified by locating the subject on each of four sliding scales. To put it in a slightly over-simplified way: does the subject incline towards introvertion or extrovertion? Sensing or intuition? Thinking or feeling? Perception or judgement? An Introverted, Intuitive, Feeling, Perceptive person would be classified INFP (the 'N' picking up the second letter of 'intuition' to avoid confusion).

Sniper instructor John C. Simpson observes that the Meyer-Briggs's Introverted, Sensing, Thinking,

RAI Model 500 Long Range Rifle

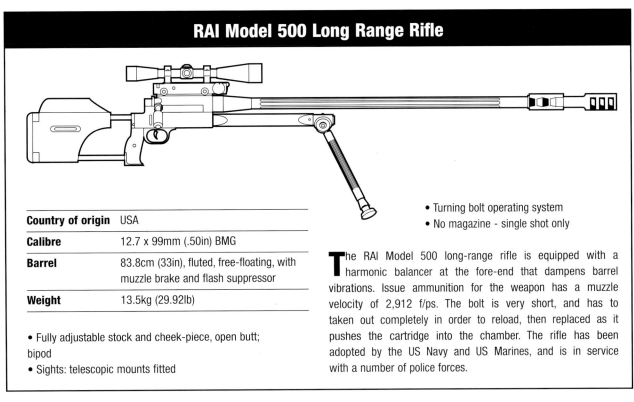

* Turning bolt operating system
* No magazine - single shot only

Country of origin	USA
Calibre	12.7 x 99mm (.50in) BMG
Barrel	83.8cm (33in), fluted, free-floating, with muzzle brake and flash suppressor
Weight	13.5kg (29.92lb)

* Fully adjustable stock and cheek-piece, open butt; bipod
* Sights: telescopic mounts fitted

The RAI Model 500 long-range rifle is equipped with a harmonic balancer at the fore-end that dampens barrel vibrations. Issue ammunition for the weapon has a muzzle velocity of 2,912 f/ps. The bolt is very short, and has to taken out completely in order to reload, then replaced as it pushes the cartridge into the chamber. The rifle has been adopted by the US Navy and US Marines, and is in service with a number of police forces.

Mauser 86SR

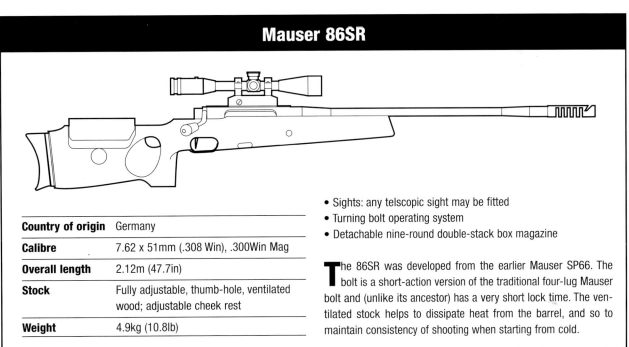

* Sights: any telscopic sight may be fitted
* Turning bolt operating system
* Detachable nine-round double-stack box magazine

Country of origin	Germany
Calibre	7.62 x 51mm (.308 Win), .300Win Mag
Overall length	2.12m (47.7in)
Stock	Fully adjustable, thumb-hole, ventilated wood; adjustable cheek rest
Weight	4.9kg (10.8lb)

The 86SR was developed from the earlier Mauser SP66. The bolt is a short-action version of the traditional four-lug Mauser bolt and (unlike its ancestor) has a very short lock time. The ventilated stock helps to dissipate heat from the barrel, and so to maintain consistency of shooting when starting from cold.

Perceptive (ISTP) type, which makes up less than 5 per cent of the population, is often referred to as the 'weapons type', but someone with that profile does not necessarily make the ideal sniper candidate. 'The ideal type is not as simple a matter as looking for introverts or singling out any single quality,' he comments, and adds wisely that talking to a certified professional is the best way to approach the interpretation of such tests, and to get the best out of them.

Several of Richard Fairburn's thoughts on sniper selection bear repeating. Fairburn notes first that a sniper candidate should have a minimum of five years' full-time service on the beat: 'This amount of experience will generally give you a solid performer long past the rashness most of us started with. A sniper's mission is one that will remove him from the action and require accurate, detailed performance without close supervision. New officers rarely possess enough deliberate, independent experience.' In the same vein, Fairburn comments:

Below: More so than his military counterpart a police sniper must be conscious of liability and 'collateral damage' and yet be prepared to fire on a 'green light' from his commander.

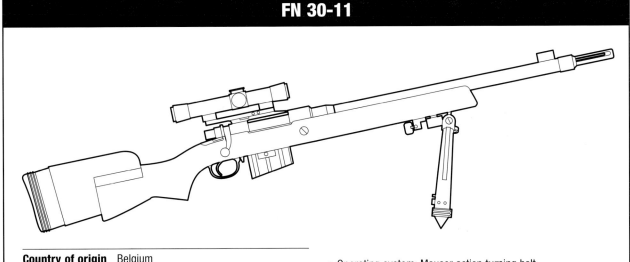

FN 30-11

Country of origin	Belgium
Calibre	7.62 x 51mm (.308 Win)
Overall length	1.11m (43.97 inches)
Barrel	50.19cm (19.76-in) heavy
Weight	4.85kg (10.69lb) empty without telescope

• Walnut stock, adjustable, using butt-spacer plates
• 4 x 28 FN telescope sights; iron sights have Anschutz aperture with adjustable dioptre

• Operating system: Mauser action turning bolt
• Magazine: 5 or 10-round detachable box

The Model 30-11 sniping FN rifle is the current sniper rifle of the Belgian and other armies, although it was intended primarily as a police and paramilitary weapon. The iron sights are click-adjustable, one click equalling 1/6 MOA adjustment capability, while the FN scope is graduated from 100m (109.3 yards) to 600m (656 yards) range. Accessories include the bipod of the MAG machine gun, butt-spacer plates, sling, and carrying case.

Sniper fire is very deliberate work, requiring detailed record keeping and nitpicking over seemingly insignificant details. When a sniper has to fire more than one shot at a felon, something went wrong, so the first shot must be perfect. For that reason, a potential sniper should be something of a perfectionist, willing to perform detailed, methodical work. Many criminal investigators make excellent snipers because they are accustomed to the slower, more exacting process of building a complicated case.

In accord with so many others, Fairburn stresses the value of hunting experience in a potential sniper, in that 'a hunter's mission is exactly like that of a trophy big-game hunter: find your quarry

without it knowing you are about, evaluate the quarry, and, if circumstances dictate, take the quarry with one well-placed shot. Hunters are also predisposed to long hours and [are] willing to face uncomfortable conditions.' But perhaps their most important edge is this: 'Hunters also have a mental advantage that is overlooked by many instructors. A big-game hunter will already have killed an animal the size of a human. Having crossed that particular threshold eliminates one potential stumbling block to performing against a live human target.'

In facing that test, the untried police officer is at one with his military counterpart. In any circumstance, sniping remains the art of killing coolly, and with a clear conscience.

CHAPTER 5

GREAT SHOTS

The sniper in action

'We have the capability to watch people die; his head explode or whatever. It's the mark of a true professional to carry out the mission'
— *Captain Steven L. Walsh, USMC*

From the appearance of the first skirmishers and sharpshooters on (and sometimes off) the battlefields of the American War of Independence, the annals of sniping have been filling with accounts of extraordinary episodes. They range from the grotesque and even farcical to astonishing feats of endurance, courage and skill at arms.

If there is anything that immediately springs to mind as defining the sniper, it's his ability to shoot accurately over extremely long distances. Every sniper who's a combat veteran, it seems, has his proud story of the 'long shot' he's taken and turned into a hit. Hunters have similar stories to tell. They're not like fishermen's tales – these quarry have actually been felled – and snipers' experiences are different yet again, because the quarry is human. The ability to handle a rifle with such coolness and aplomb in the midst of great danger is yet another testimony to the depth of inner resources that successful snipers possess.

THE LONG SHOT

One of the most remarkable feats of long-range shooting – especially given the limits of the available

Left: Finland has given the world some of the best hunting and sniping rifles and, during World War II, Simo Häyhäe and Suko Kolkka together accounted for over 900 Russians.

Whitworth Rifle

- 730m (800-yard) range
- Muzzle-loading single-shot operating system

Country of origin	United Kingdom
Calibre	11.43mm (.45-inch ball)
Overall length	1.25m (49 inches)
Weight	4.05kg (8lb 15 1/8oz)

- Almost fully stocked in oak or walnut, with iron fittings
- Side-mounted Davidson telescopic sight, plus iron sights

Fired by Queen Victoria to inaugurate the British National Rifle Association's Wimbledon match in 1860, the Whitworth was a rival to the Enfield. Although extensively tested and troop-trialled in 1862 and 1863, it was never adopted. The essential difference between the two weapons was that the Whitworth was polygonal-bored instead of rifled, giving excellent accuracy, and making it popular as a target rifle.

Riflemen, ATTENTION !

A COMPANY OF ONE HUNDRED MEN to be selected from the

BEST RIFLE SHOTS,

In the State, is to be raised to act as a *COMPANY OF SHARP SHOOTERS* through the War. Each man will be entitled to

A BOUNTY OF $22,00,

When mustered into the service of the United States, and

100,00 DOLLARS

at the close of the War, in addition to his regular pay.

No man will be accepted or mustered into service who is not an active and able bodied man, and who cannot when firing at a rest at a distance of two hundred yards, put ten consecutive shots into a target the average distance not to exceed five inches from the centre of the bull's eye to the centre of the ball : and all candidates will have to pass such an examination as to satisfy the recruiting officer of their fitness for enlistment in this corps.

Recruits having Rifles to which they are accustomed are requested to bring them to the place of rendezvous.

Recruits will be received by   JAMES D. FESSENDEN,
Adams Block, No. 23, Market Square, PORTLAND, Maine.

Sept. 16, 1861.

technology – occurred in 1864 during the American Civil War and was inflicted by a now anonymous Confederate lieutenant on a number of Union staff officers.

As Captain F.S. Harris recalls in his book, *Confederate Veteran*, a party of horseman were spotted riding up to high ground far in the rear of the Federal lines. A lieutenant who was among those watching from the Confederate side asked a passing captain of engineers to calculate the distance. The the reply was 2250 yards (2060m). At this point, one of the Federals, who looked like he might be a general, could be seen riding ahead from the group and stopping at the highest point in the landscape. The Confederate lieutenant took a Whitworth rifle, trained the gun on him with a globe sight, aimed and fired.

The officer fell from his horse, and his staff gathered around him quickly. Two more shots were

Left: A Civil War recruiting poster calls for 'best rifle shots' to join the Maine Regiment. It stipulates achievement of 10 shots within five inches of the bull at 200 yards.

fired in rapid succession, and three men were carried from that place. A few days later a Northern paper announced that General – I forget the name – and several of his staff were killed by Rebel sharpshooters at long range.

If the range was accurately estimated, this must be one of the most extraordinary series of shots of all time. At even half the distance this would remain an amazing achievement, and had to call for as much judgement as luck.

Chance combinations of shooter, rifle, ballistics and wind can produce results that seem unbelievable. During the early part of World War I German snipers gained a reputation for fearsome accuracy, a reputation that was not always entirely deserved. Nevertheless, many British soldiers had reason to respect the abilities of their opponents. Frank Richards, who served in the Royal Welch Fusiliers for the duration of the war, described the bizarre results of German sharpshooting mixed with random events:

We used to fix iron plates in the parapet of our trench, concealing them as cleverly as we could, but in a day or two the enemy generally discovered them and would rattle bullets all around ... The hole in the iron plate was just large enough to put the muzzle of the rifle through, and one morning I saw the greatest shooting feat that I ever saw during the whole of the war. A man named Blacktin was firing from behind one of these plates. He had fired two rounds and was just about to pull the trigger to fire the third when he seemed to be hurled against the back of the trench, the rifle falling from his hands. A German sniper had fired and his bullet had entered the barrel of Blacktin's rifle, where it was now lodged fast, splitting the top end of the barrel the same way as a man would peel a banana. Blacktin's shoulder was badly bruised. [*Old Soldiers Never Die*, Anthony Mott, 1983, 62]

World War II saw snipers operating in almost every conceivable climate, condition and campaign, but proven approaches rarely failed. As one US Marine veteran tells the story, during the battles to capture Saipan in June 1944, the classic unassuming,

Right: Major General John F. Reynolds was one of a number of senior officers, mostly of the Union side, to be killed by a sniper's bullet in the American Civil War.

patient, but supremely self-confident approach typical of the seasoned sniper freed a unit caught by an enemy in a superior position:

We were pinned down on the beach at Saipan by a machine gun bunker. The pill box commanded a sweeping view of the area, and there was just no way we could get at it. Plenty of our boys had died trying.

Finally one of our 90-day wonders [a freshly qualified officer] got on the horn and requested a sniper. A few minutes later, I saw two old gunnery sergeants sashaying towards us, wearing shooting jackets and campaign hats! As soon as I saw these Smokey Bears bobbing over to us, I figured this could be some show. And it was.

These two old sergeants skinnied up to the lieutenant and just asked him to point out the

bunker. Then they unfolded two shooting mats, took off their Smokey Bears and settled down to business. One manned a spotter's scope while the other fired a 1903 Springfield with a telescopic sight rig.

That bunker must have been 1100 or 1200 yards [1000–1100m] away, but in just a few minutes, with three or four spotting rounds, this old gunny on the Springfield slipped a round right into the bunker's firing slit. One dead machine gunner. But their commander just stuck another man on that gun. Our sniper shot him, too. After the fourth man bit a slug, I think they got the idea. We moved up on their flank and destroyed the bunker while our snipers kept the machine gun silent. Then the two gunnys dusted themselves off, rolled up their mats and settled their Smokey Bears back on their heads. And just

Springfield M1903

Country of origin	USA
Calibre	7.62mm (.30-'06)
Overall length	1.09m (43.25 inches)
Barrel length	60.9cm (24 inches)
Weight	3.9kg (8lb 11oz)

- One-piece Mauser-type shoulder stock and fore-end, with separate top handguard secured by barrel band and nose cap
- Front blade sight, rear ladder graduated to 1830m (2000 yards); various telescopic sights
- Turning-bolt operating system
- Integral five-round box magazine, top-loaded

The USA adopted their best turning-bolt service rifle in 1903, and with the ammunition changes adopted in 1906 (the -'06 of the calibre refers to this date, not to a measure of the bore), this was their main service rifle for World War I. The Springfield is another variant of the Mauser.

The first modification of this rifle, the M1903A1 was a change to the shape of the stock from the straight Mauser type to one with a pronounced pistol grip. The US Marine sniper version used in the Pacific theatre of World War II was fitted with an 8x Unertl scope. Further modifications to simplify production were designated the M1903A3, and the A4 variant of this rifle was issued for sniping. This is essentially the M1903A3 rifle fitted with a 4x Weaver telescopic sight on a receiver mount, and an improved bolt action. This weapon saw service in Europe in World War II, and in the Korean War.

moseyed away. [Quoted by James A. Dunnigan, 'The American Sniper', in *Guns & Ammo Annual* 1981, p51–52.]

SNIPING IN THE BACKYARDS

Nearly a quarter of a century later, in Vietnam, sniper Thomas D. Ferran (later a USMC light colonel) amassed a score of 41 confirmed kills. But in the early days he also found he had to persuade his fellow Marines that snipers were a real and useful infantry resource. By the usual combination of good fortune and his own skill, he made his first kill under the eyes of fellow Marines on his first mission.

Above: A Marine sniper in the Solomon Islands aims his Springfield from 'a front line outpost'. The discarded tin can certainly does not suggest a well-prepared hide.

Having just arrived on a hill south of Chu Lai in January 1967 Ferran was getting ready for the next day's patrol when he and his partner spotted a Viet Cong guerrilla digging on a fairly distant hill in a free-fire zone. They knew that what he was digging was a 'spider hole' from which to fire on a patrol some day.

I'd trained to fire out to 1100 metres [1200 yards], and when I graduated I had to be able to put a bullet into a ten-inch [25cm] circle eight out of ten times at that range. I knew the VC was at about 1300 meters [1425 yards] because it was two more football fields beyond the 1100 meters range we had trained on. At these long ranges the wind became a major problem. In the end I had to dead-reckon. I said to [my partner] Pee-Wee, 'I'm going to aim this shot high and right, over this guy's head. I want you to spot for me.'

Meanwhile, unbeknownst to me, there was a group of Marines coming around to look at us. I was getting ready to fire my best shot. I had a perfect rifle and this was my first shot since graduating. I fired and missed. Pee-Wee had put the binoculars a quarter-turn out of focus so he could read the wind and follow the bullet trail going down to the target and see it impact. Pee-Wee called that I was low and to the left, about five and five. So I put the cross-hairs right there. When I fired that first shot and the bullet missed, the guy just looked up and couldn't believe he was being shot at. He took cover but resumed his duties within a few minutes.

When I hit him with my second shot, there was applause from the guys around me. We were elated because we were trying to sell sniping to the infantry, and here they could see that the concept of sniping could work.

During the battle for Hue during the Tet offensive of 1968, Jeffrey Clifford's successful 'long shot' seems to have been effected by a like partnership of skill and luck:

My 'long shot' (+1400 yards [1280m]) was courtesy of Hue. Most would say it was not a probable accomplishment, and I admit that I had fired at least 10 rounds at these same NVAs straight up the boulevard on the other side of the river without success. Finally I found a forlorn lieutenant belonging to a tank group and borrowed his range finder. No wonder I was missing, I was estimating 400 yards [365m] short.

The NVAs were moving gear in and around a large pagoda approximately 20 feet [6m] high. I put the crosshairs several feet above the pagoda roof and fired. Regas (my ATL – Assistant Team Leader) could not see a strike so I told him to get some tracers from a nearby bull gun team. With Regas spotting I fired again. Perhaps it was the luck of the Irish, but we all (the Lt was still hanging around, looking through his binocs) observed the tracer's high arc and saw it enter an NVA just below his neckline. He went down as if the proverbial ton of bricks had fallen on him. The Lieutenant was excited enough to bring over a captain who looked through the scope to verify the heap. Ah well, chalk one up to luck. [Sergeant Jeffrey L. Clifford, 'In His Own Words' in Chandler and Chandler, *Death From Afar*, Volume II (Iron Brigade Armory, Maryland), p. 45]

In the first few years of the IRA's attempted insurrection in Northern Ireland, all the factions' paramilitaries and the British Army used snipers extensively. An outstanding instance of army marksmanship in Northern Ireland occurred in this period, in Londonderry in 1972. The shooter was – unusually, for sniping has become something of an NCO preserve – an officer and a prize-winning Bisley shot.

This officer found himself nearby when a Ferret armoured car of the Blues and Royals was ambushed approaching a roundabout on the Foyle road coming into Londonderry. It was blown up by a mine, and an IRA ambush party was on hand to fire on the vehicle. Arriving at the scene he started to look in the area of the gunfire for targets. 'That's when he saw a car drive down Coach Road. It suddenly stopped in the middle of the road, and two

Right: Just as in the Pacific theatre, the jungles of southeast Asia were a fertile sniping ground for both sides. This 'Vietnam' scene was in fact part of a counter-guerrilla training exercise undertaken on Okinawa in 1962.

men got out and began unloading weapons. More men arrived to join the ambush and they began to take the weapons from the armoury car.'

According to the map, these men were 1100m (1200 yards) away. That would mean a flight time of two or three seconds between squeezing the trigger and the bullet hitting the target – the wind was going to be a real problem. However, because an IRA lead-

er had just died, the area was hung with black flags.

…it was like being on Century range at Bisley; I had the flags all the way down, and I could read them all off. So I made my estimation as to what the wind correction was for 1100 metres…I was off the scale for the wind allowances in my sniper pocket book, but we had trained ourselves in 1000

L96A1 – Accuracy International PM

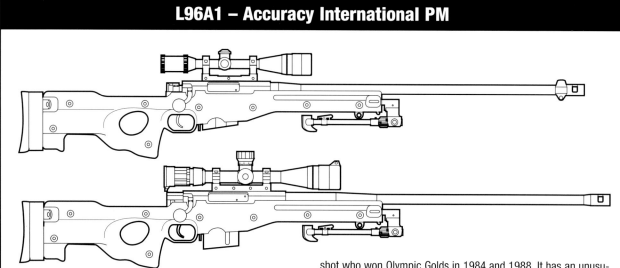

Country of origin	United Kingdom
Calibre	7.62 x 51mm (.3 x 2 inches) or 8.585mm (.338 Lapua Magnum)
Overall length	1.13–1.19m (44.25–47 inches)
Barrel length	61cm (24 inches)
Weight, without telescope	6.5kg (14 lb 6oz)

• Composite stock
• Schmidt & Bender 6x or 10x sights
• Turning-bolt operating system
• Detachable 10- or 12-round box magazine

The L96A1 has a maximum effective range of 1000m (1090 yards) and is the British Army designation of the standard AWC PM. The rifle was built under the supervision of UK rifle shooter Malcolm Cooper, a smallbore (.22) 3-positional target

shot who won Olympic Golds in 1984 and 1988. It has an unusual set-up the stock is in two pieces, which bolt onto a sub-chassis. The action is glued and screwed to this sub-chassis. The barrel is free-floating.

In a Ministry of Defence competition, the L96A1 narrowly beat the Parker-Hale M85 to become the standard sniper rifle. The PM uses an aluminium frame over which is placed a high-impact plastic stock. An adjustable Parker Hale Bi-Pod is fitted as standard, while an adjustable spring-loaded monopod is housed in the butt. An uprated version, the AW, features improvements that include an easier bolt action, frost-proof mechanism, muzzle brake and a 10 x 42 Hensoldt telescopic sight. Other Accuracy International-related models in use include the AWP Counter-Terrorist Rifle, AWS Covert Sniper Rifle (with integral sound suppressor, using subsonic ammunition), and the SM Super Magnum Sniper Rifle (available in .338-inch Lapua Magnum, .300 Winchester Magnum or 7mm Remington Magnum). This last is intended for anti-personnel sniping at ranges of 900m (1000 yards), and for destroying light armour and other equipment.

metres [1100 yards] shooting while on the sniper course ... [But] I'll be frank with you, the first chap I knocked down I had actually got the wind slightly wrong ... because of the time of flight he moved away from the car, and just walked straight into the bullet. And that was it, down and out.

This sniper fire was masked by fire from infantry sent in to rescue the Ferret crew. The terrorists were unaware of where it was coming from.

So at first they assumed they were being hit from further down the road, and kept on coming down. We had one terrorist in the bushes on the side, and we had another wounded under a car. During the engagement I fired some 43 rounds and my sniper partner 40 rounds. Subsequently, from intelligence sources, it would appear that we had knocked down 10 terrorists. Seven were credited to me and three to my sergeant.

They reckon my furthest target was over 1300 metres, 1344 meters [1470 yards] to be precise. This was a shot I took much further up the road. We were very much at the limit of our equipment, especially in terms of the sight, which was only X4 magnification. Initially no one could believe we could hit them at that ranges over 1000 metres, so I was being asked on the brigade net what type of weapon I was using, at the very moment I was trying to take out targets. The CO eventually got them off my back by explaining that we had just won the sniper championship at Bisley and that our skills and weapons were equal to the task.

We continued firing at the terrorists whenever a target appeared. One of them dashed across the road, and we saw him go through a doorway. My

sergeant fired a shot but we thought we were too late. Subsequently we discovered that having gone through the doorway, he slammed the door and put his back against it, no doubt thinking, 'Thank God for that!' At that moment the bullet hit the door. When we looked later we saw a perfect oblong broadside-on hole going through; the bullet had taken most of the chap's chest away.

After this engagement, the level of IRA activity in Londonderry dropped noticeably for a time.

Right: This British Paratoop Regiment sniper, seen securing an airfield during an exercise, is using an L42A1 – a modified version of the Lee Enfield Mk 4(T) first introduced during World War II and gradually replaced by more modern rifles.

ALL TOGETHER NOW

While the archetypal sniper action involves the military equivalent of the 'lone gunman' exercising all the cunning, dedication and skill he can muster, there is no lack of classic sniping incidents in which more than one rifle was involved. It's the sniper's business to be flexible in his approach to any given (especially unexpected) situation, and in some circumstances another eye and another barrel (or two) can save the day.

Clifford Shore tells of one such episode during World War II, just before the battle for Caen in 1944. A Scottish battalion was holding a position known as the 'Triangle' and was regularly harassed by mortar fire. The battalion sniping section had found a ready-made hide in a wrecked German armoured car in No Man's Land, where each day at noon one sniper team relieved the pair on watch.

On this particular sector the slightest movement invariably resulted in a fairly severe mortar 'stonking' and since it was clearly evident that our positions could not be seen from the ground level, it was realized that the Hun must have an observer up aloft – in a tree ... The midday relief had just been effected and the two snipers going off-duty were crawling back to our lines when a low whistle and whispered injunction halted them and caused them to recrawl the 10 yards [9m] or so they had covered back to the post. One of the relieving snipers, bringing fresh eyes to the job, had spotted the German observer; he was high in a tree, excellently camouflaged, but he had made the most elementary mistake of lighting a cigarette – no doubt it was a case of 'familiar contempt'. A whispered conversation between the four snipers followed as to the range of the German observer; they could not

Right: Sniper fire pins down an American patrol, Normandy 1944. Few snipers worth their salt would fall for the bait the nearest soldier offers. The broken MG42 in the foreground may even have been left by the sniper to attract curious GIs.

agree. Two of them said they estimated the range to be between 250 and 300 yards [230–75m]; the others said it was nearer 350 yards [320m]. The matter was settled in a rather novel manner. Three of the snipers set their sights at 250, 300 and 350, whilst the fourth sniper took the binoculars and kept them riveted on the prospective target. When quite satisfied he coolly gave the three men a fire order; the three rifles 'spoke as one' and the Bosche came somersaulting to the ground.

In the Korean War in the early 1950s, US Marine Gunnery Sergeant Francis H. Killeen found the assistance of those wielding the Browning Automatic Rifle (BAR) invaluable, while he used his special skill to mark their targets. Killeen was issued with a M1903A4 Springfield rifle fitted with an 8x Unertl telescopic sight. This is how he was introduced to life as a sniper:

Our first real chance to use the sniper rifles came at Su Dong Ni where our battalion was rushed up to the front and thrown headlong into a fire fight against a Chinese regiment.

We got into a ditch alongside the road, and I immediately figured our range would be 400 yards [365m] uphill. I looked through my 8-power scope and could spot an otherwise unseen line of riflemen firing down at us by seeing the 'fuzz' of their projectiles. Lieutenant Davis, our 60mm mortar man, was right beside me. I told him where the enemy fire was coming from and in less than a minute he had three mortars in action and the fire lifted. We attacked and took the positions.

This was the first time I found my sniper gun to be more effective than my M1 rifle. Usually we were in close actions where the M1's rapid fire could be more important than the long range capability, but this time we were looking over a big valley at ridges 500 to 600 yards [460–550m] across the way. I chose a

rock on the far ridge and got my lieutenant to spot my strikes with his binoculars. In that way, I made sure my rifle was still shooting where I aimed.

In the late afternoon, columns of enemy began moving into position for evening festivities. I got off a couple of rounds, but without a spotter I could not tell if I was making hits. I got a BAR man to register his rifle on the same rock I had used for zeroing. When he had his sights right we tried some team shooting.

When I located enemy I fired tracer at him or them. Although tracer is lighter than the AP we were using, the trajectory was close enough and the BAR man, who could not see the enemy soldiers with his iron sights, simply attempted to catch my tracer with his bullets. The idea was to hammer the enemy with a decent volume of fire in the hopes that if I missed, the BAR man would get him.

The technique was instantly popular, and I soon had a light machine gun and two more

BARs creating the biggest beaten zone I ever saw. My lieutenant, James Stemple, 3rd Platoon A-1-7, got more riflemen into the fray, and we had the enemy falling all along their wood line.

In the heat of the action, and with the obvious success we were enjoying, I forgot about the 'hit and run' rule. We have to remember that the other guys also have people who can shoot. A bullet about one click low reminded me, and I cleared out just as a few more came into where I had just been. [Gunnery Sgt Francis H. Killeen, 'Sniping: Notes from a Career Marine' in N.A. Chandler and Roy Chandler, *Death From Afar*, Volume IV (Iron Brigade Armory, Maryland)]

William H. Dabney, then a captain in the 3rd Battalion, 26th US Marines, was at the siege of Khe Sanh in northwestern Viet Nam in 1968. Dabney had been ordered to hold a position preyed on by a sniper. He used what was to hand to deal with his problem. The results were not without psychological interest.

The sniper was well concealed on a hill about 400 yards [365m] to the north, the only ground high enough and close enough to our positions on Hill 881 South to offer a vantage point for effective rifle fire. He had been there for about a week. He fired rarely but he was deadly. With a total of perhaps 20 rounds, he had killed two of my Marines and wounded half-a-dozen others. Even a napalm storm failed to silence him. He had my stretcher bearers pinned down at a time when I had some serious medevacing to be getting on with. He was careful, but not quite careful enough. On a still afternoon, a machine gunner spotted a slight movement in a bush. A recoilless rifle, our primary mid-range anti-tank gun, was

Left: In Korea, the Marines refined the concept of the sniper/observer team – the observer calling the fall of shot and helping select targets and threats. Modern practice calls for more separation in combat than shown here.

zeroed in on his spider hole and a 106mm high-explosive plastic round was sent crashing through the bush. The NVA nest became a crater, and its former occupant a formless pulp. Another sniper sprang up from nowhere to take his place. He too got a 106. The sniping continued for 10 days – this time from a different part of the hill. Again the crew wrestled their 106 around the rough slopes. When the gunner and spotter picked their mark, a young private crawled towards me.

Crouched in his foxhole, he had been watching this particular sniper for the past week. The guy had fired about as many rounds as his predecessors, but hadn't hit a damned thing. The private suggested we leave him be for the time being. If we blew him away, the North Vietnamese might replace him with someone who shot straight. This idea made sense and the 106 was moved back. My men even started waving 'Maggies' drawers' at him – a red cloth that we used to sig-

Left: US Marines in Beirut return fire at one of the many armed factions that threatened their bases. As related here, the best way to deal with a 'sniper' firing a heavy machine-gun can be to use the same level of firepower in return.

complicating the issue no end – had been invaded the previous year by Israeli forces. Corporal Tom Rutter reached Beirut with the US Marine 1/8 Battalion Landing Team in June 1983. The Marine snipers were eventually permitted to return the constant fire from Muslim gunmen in the maze of buildings called Hooterville, which faced the Marines' base. Rutter recalled their first action, which involved some effective work with an M60 machine-gun crew, specialists not usually associated with sniping.

> I had just assumed watch on the roof [of the base building] with Corporal Baldree and was making my first sniper's log entry after examining through binoculars the parapets and fortifications that surrounded us. '1730 hours,' I wrote. 'All quiet. No new obstacles or positions.' I peered out. Hooterville was almost dark, although all the light had not yet drained out of the sky. Maybe the ragheads had already heard we had turned and were going to shoot back.
>
> Suddenly, a string of bullets screamed over our heads above the sandbags as a heavy machine gun opened up from somewhere at the edge of Hooterville. I ducked instinctively. So did Baldree. We grinned sheepishly at each other as the next burst of machine gun fire chewed viciously at the sandbags.
>
> We darted from one firing port to another, taking quick looks out, trying to locate the nest. Every few seconds the machine gun snapped a few rounds at us. The rounds were hitting near the firing openings in the sandbags, but so far none of the bullets had come through. I didn't want my head framed in an opening when the gunner finally hit it.
>
> 'I don't see a goddamned thing,' Baldree cried in exasperation.

nal a miss on the rifle range. Then we figured he might be faking us and we quit the taunts. He stayed there for the whole of the battle – about two months – fired regularly, and never hit a man.

BY ANY MEANS NECESSARY

In 1983, US Marines were deployed along with French and Italian troops to Beirut, Lebanon, as part of a UN attempt to bring about a ceasefire between warring factions in the then lawless nation, which –

'Wait ...' I said. 'Okay ... The tall building at two o'clock. See it? Second floor. The dude knows his stuff. He's not firing from the window. He's back in the shadows.'

'I see him!' Baldree hooted as quick, flickering muzzle flashes lit up the room. We were watching through scopes and binoculars.

'He's too far back in the room, 'Baldree said. 'We can't get his angle from here.'

I had a thought. 'No, but we can double-team the shitbird.'

I grabbed the field phone and got Crumley who was on watch at the grunts' concrete barrier on the ground floor. I quickly outlined the plan to him. Baldree and I would mark the window with rifle tracers, if the grunts would follow up with their M60 machine gun. We finally had a chance to fight back. I didn't want our first raghead getting away.

I checked the range with the mil-dot scale in my rifle scope. It was about six hundred yards [550m]. Two tracers streaked across the field in the gathering darkness like swift angry bees. They plunged through the enemy machine gunner's window, clearly marking it for the Marines below. Larger, angrier bees followed as the M60 on the ground floor sent a stream of tracers through the same window. The M60 pumped the distant room full of lead. Tracers trapped inside the concrete room ricocheted insanely in a weird kind of light-and-shadow show. My entries into the sniper's log for the rest of the night read simply: All Quiet. [Corporal Tom Rutter, quoted in Charles W. Sasser and Craig Roberts, *One Shot – One Kill* (Pocket Books, 1990) pp. 234–36]

In Viet Nam, early in 1970, US Marine Joseph T. Ward was a sniper squad leader at Hill 65 at An Hoa. Ward had been trained as both scout and sniper in the Marine tradition and had had no hesitation in calling up air and artillery strikes when it was clearly beyond his capacity to handle the enemy forces facing him. On one occasion, as dawn broke, he and

his spotter, Lance Corporal Terry Lightfoot, who was armed with an M14, saw at least a company, possibly a battalion, of North Vietnamese army (NVA) regulars break cover from the treeline opposite their hide and begin crossing the open ground towards them. The snipers were clearly about to be overrun. Ward contacted air control. Fortunately, two F-4 Phantoms armed with napalm happened to be just seven minutes from the target area. The fast movers were redirected to Ward's position. While the jets headed toward them, Ward and Lightfoot prepared to shake up the advancing NVA troops, firing at long range to hold them in the rice paddies and along the tree line, so making them an ideal target for the Phantoms. Ward recounted:

Lightfoot was laying M14 magazines in front of him so he could get to them more easily. I was heartened to see that he had the instinct to know that we were about to get into an out-and-out shooting match. He'd never tangled with that many enemy troops; neither had I. They could overwhelm us by sheer numbers, but we had the element of surprise, marksmanship, and concealment on our side. I looked at my watch with one eye and at Charlie with the other through the rifle scope. They had started moving, and the lead man would be within Lightfoot's 700-yard [640m] limit in less than 60 seconds.

'Now!' I shouted at Lightfoot. He began firing, and at the same moment I shot a machine gunner between the eyes. Lightfoot hit the three lead men before they could all take cover. My next shot took out the second machine gunner. My third hit a mortar man in the neck. Shot four hit the second mortar man; just as he dropped a round down the tube, he fell over like a rag doll and the result of his last act as a soldier was a misplaced mortar that landed among his own people who Lightfoot had pinned down, killing two of them. They thought it was from us and that we'd hit them with mortars too. When they moved, Lightfoot dropped two more.

My fifth shot hit the ammo man starting to take over the first machine gun.

AK rounds were hitting the hillside randomly. The North Vietnamese hadn't located Ward and Lightfoot yet, but it seemed they had to eventually. So long as Lightfoot was doing such a good job of pinning down what was left of the forward squad, though, Ward could forget about them and look back at the second gun. Since it was out of action, he moved his scope back to the first, just as it began to belch smoke. In his haste to get back on the radio and listen for Big Ten (the call sign of the lead F-4), he missed with his sixth shot.

'Son of a Bitch!' I yelled, as I picked up the handset with one hand and began to reload with

Above: In Vietnam, ambush of patrols was a constant danger, as was sniping from the abundant forest cover. A platoon's own sniper team was a useful asset who could locate the enemy and, if necessary, call in artillery or air support.

the other. 'Come on Big Ten,' I thought, while I chambered a round and put the first of five rounds into the magazine.

Lightfoot was methodically, calmly, firing at the men trapped in the rice paddy. I was glad I wasn't one of them. He wiped the sweat from his eyes and swore once when a bullet hit close enough to kick dirt in his face. Other than that he said nothing.

Charlie had both guns going and was raking the side of our hill with unnerving precision. I watched as tracers ricocheted in increasing numbers nearer and nearer to our position and wondered if I had cut it too close.

I'd just put in round number four when I heard the voice of an angel over the radio. 'Long Rifle [Ward's call sign], this is Big Ten. I'm on final approach. Over and out.'

I looked through the scope in the direction I expected Big Ten to be coming from. He was barely visible, but right on the money. Twenty more seconds, that's all we needed. I put in the

last round and switched back to the trees and shot a third machine gunner brought into action. Charlie was making too much noise trying to find us to hear Big Ten coming, and the jets were almost on them. I had time for one more shot and took out a mortar man, when the rockets and guns of Big Ten got Charlie's attention. Seconds later the tree line erupted in flames and black smoke. All enemy fire in our direction stopped, the only sounds were from Lightfoot, still working over those poor bastards in the rice field, and the faint roar of napalm devouring trees and humans. [Joseph T. Ward, *Dear Mom: A Sniper's Vietnam*, Ivy Books 1991, p151]

Below: Marines train 'scout-snipers' whose reconnaissance role is as important as that of the sharpshooter. Here a Marine of the 2nd Bn, 9th Marine regiment checks the opposite treeline for enemy activity before his company crosses the open paddy fields.

Not content with that, Ward radioed the artillery fire controllers at An Hoa, who then carpeted the area with a bombardment from batteries of 105mm and 175mm guns. While this barrage was churning up the NVA, Ward and Lightfoot slipped from their hide and made their way back to base. The two men had been instrumental in savaging an entire NVA battalion.

EXTREME MEASURES

As Joseph Ward's account shows, not every successful sniping operation ends in a shot from a rifle barrel. From time to time it's necessary to call on larger and heavier resources, be they a co-operative artillery battery or a flight of fast-mover strike aircraft. As a particularly sophisticated incarnation of the military forward observer, the sniper should regard it as no skin off his nose to recognise when the odds are overwhelming, and coarser, more brutal measures are needed.

Occasionally, sniping has been carried out with artillery.

Fighting the Japanese in the Pacific theatre during World War II, Russell Braddon, an Australian artilleryman, witnessed this summary disposal of an enemy sniper by means almost as drastic:

> I was amazed to see a fellow gunner raise a heavy Boys anti-tank rifle to his shoulder, aim high and fire. He was at once flung backwards, whilst the half-inch shell most certainly passed harmlessly into the stratosphere. When I reached him he was rubbing his shattered right shoulder and swearing softly but with that consummate fluency which is the prerogative of the Australian farmer who is perpetually harassed by the cussedness of things inanimate.
>
> 'What the hell are you trying to do, Harry?' I asked.
>
> 'Get that bloody sniper up the top of that bloody tree,' he replied tersely. It appeared that, fired off the ground, the Boys rifle had not sufficient elevation to hit a tree high up. However, since the sniper fired from behind the top of the tree trunk he could only be shot through it – a Boys rifle was, therefore, essential for the job. We decided to do it together. With the barrel resting on my shoulder, the butt against his own. Harry took a long aim, apparently quite undeterred by the bursts of bullets from all sides, which our stance attracted. I was not in the least undeterred. In fact, as we stood there, our feet spread wide apart to take some of the shock, I was very deterred indeed. Then Harry fired and I was crushed to the ground and Harry was flung against a tree and the sniper toppled gracelessly out from behind his tree, thudding on to the earth below, and our job was done. I left Harry, still swearing volubly and rubbing his shoulder, and crept back to the line of men I now knew so well. [Russell Braddon, *The Naked Island*, T. Laurie 1952, p77]

ONE ON ONE

Counter-sniping, pitting one sniper against another, is perhaps the deadliest game of all, and it always has been. The Dardanelles (Gallipoli) campaign of World War I saw a duel between ace snipers, one of them Australian, the other Turkish.

The Australian – veteran kangaroo hunter Billy Sing – had already experienced the perils of his calling when his observer, Trooper Tom Sheehan, was shot. Sing had achieved considerable publicity for an impressive tally of kills (his final score was officially 150, but probably far higher), and the Turks were determined to stop him. An enemy marksman spotted the snipers' hide and fired: the bullet passed straight through Sheehan's telescope. Fortunately he didn't have the scope to his eye, but he was wounded in both hands before the bullet entered his mouth and exited his left cheek. Almost spent, it then struck Sing in the right shoulder. Sing was out of action for a week, recovering. When he reappeared, he had a more formidable opponent.

Already decorated by the Sultan for his proficiency, Sing's adversary – whom the Australians dubbed

'Abdul the Terrible' – brought the professional vigour of a forensic scientist to his task of locating and eliminating the Australian.

'There was,' says one account, 'an inexplicable ability by the Turks to separate the indiscriminate good fortune of some of the Anzac shooters from the true craftsmanship of the sniper Sing.' Abdul was fed only reports of fatalities that were 'confidently assessed' as having been Sing's work. The Turk reconstructed each incident, working out the bullet's trajectory from the entry and exit wounds and from the position and stance of the victim at the moment

of impact, as described by witnesses. From what he learned, he could estimate where the shooter of the bullet was located.

Sing, for all his shooting prowess, had made the cardinal error of not moving his hide – and Abdul the Terrible eventually fixed on the spot, a small rise on the heights of the area known as Chatham's Post. Then, in the dark, he built his own hide. He spent days in it simply watching, ignoring all other targets lest he give his position away. He was waiting for Sing to reveal himself. Eventually his persistence paid off.

One morning, as the Australians settled into the position Abdul had discovered, Sing's observer did his usual frontal sweep with the telescope. He whispered immediately that they had had a target. When

Below: In the Gallipoli campaign in 1915, in the lulls between attacks, artillery and sniper fire were the greatest danger to both sides. King of the ANZAC snipers was the Australian Billy Sing.

Sing took the telescope, he found himself staring into the face – and rifle-muzzle – of Abdul the Terrible.

Sing took up his rifle, and the Turk watched as the Australian gently eased the loophole cover back and cautiously pushed the weapon forward. As Abdul prepared to squeeze the trigger, however, Sing's bullet struck him between the eyes.

The next time the Turks discovered Billy Sing, they saved their men and called in heavy artillery instead. The first round landed with almost pinpoint accuracy. But it fell short enough – and there were seconds enough before a second shell completely

Above: In the Pacific theatre of World War II some of the most effective snipers were also Australians, many of whom were kangaroo hunters and knew a thing or two about hitting a living, man-sized target.

destroyed the emplacement – for Billy and his colleague to escape.

Clifford Shore, having become acquainted with Australian snipers of the next generation operating in World War II, explained their uncanny ability thus:

Some of the Australian snipers were really remarkable shots and probably the best of them

were the kangaroo hunters. The majority of these men had been members of rifle clubs in Australia, where they used the .303 rifle with the heavy barrel which is so popular in that country and which is very accurate over long and short ranges alike. Australian snipers were trained to engage targets at longer ranges than the British sniper.

Like all hunters for skins, European chamois hunters, Russian squirrel hunters and Canadian trappers, the Australian kangaroo hunters have to be extremely careful where they put their bullets. A hole in the centre of the back, though it would kill the animal, would certainly have an economic detriment to the pelt. A good [kangaroo] hunter aims low, near to the root of the big tail, a shot which is nearly always certain to break the spinal cord, or high up under the forearms at the heart. Some of the best men prefer the head, maintaining that a brain shot is the most effective in bringing down the quarry, and despatching it humanely. Probably the reason why the kangaroo hunter made such a damned good sniper was that if he is to earn good money he must kill cleanly every time he fires. The kangaroo is not a nervous beast, and at the first few cracks of rifle fire a feeding herd will pause momentarily and then proceed with the important job in hand. The fact that one or two of their number collapse on the ground occasions no panic or concern since a kangaroo is an animal which lies down for a great deal of its time ... One hunter will frequently make a bag of twenty or more before the mob takes flight. But a vastly different story would be told if the hunter merely wounded with his first shot; a bucking, thrashing kangaroo would alarm the whole quarry, and the hunter would not be worthy of his title.

Left: Stalingrad became something of a sniper's playground for both sides. Popular targets were soldiers returning to their positions with water or supplies, the lack of which had an effect on morale out of proportion to the loss of a single soldier.

In Timor one of these kangaroo hunters had a great sporting time, and whether right or wrong, he played sportingly with the Japs, and never used his telescopic sight on his rifle when the Nips were at less than 300 yards [275m] range! He was credited with 47 Japanese killed but with characteristic modesty claimed only 25 certainties, remarking that 'In my game you can't count a 'roo unless you see him drop and know exactly where to go to skin him.'

And one 'roo hunter presented with a mass target of automaton Japs – the type of target that comes once only in the life of one sniper in a hundred – got twelve of the yellow-men in twelve shots in fifteen minutes. Some shooting!

NATIONAL CHAMPIONS DUEL

During the German Army's siege of Stalingrad, which began in late 1942, the ruined city became a kind of sniper's playground or heaven, if there can be such a thing. The Red Army's star sniper was Vasili Zaitsev, a hunter from the Ural Mountains, who had killed over 100 Germans by the end of September 1942 and had set up his own sniping school in the wreckage of the city's Lazur chemicals factory. He had an epic man-to-man engagement with an enemy sniper sent specifically to eliminate him. Zaitsev's commanding officer, General V.I. Chuikov, writes:

I met many of the well-known snipers, like Vasili Zaitsev, Anatoli Chekhov and Viktor Medvedev; I talked to them, helped them as far as I could and frequently consulted them. These well-known soldiers were not distinguished in any particular way from the others. Quite the reverse. When I first met Zaitsev and Medvedev, I was struck by their modesty, the leisurely way they moved, their particular placid temperament, the attentive way they looked at things; they could look at the same object for a long time without blinking. They

Mosin Nagant M1891 rifle

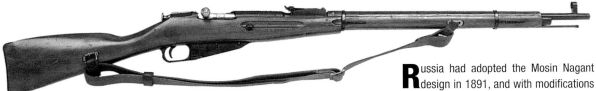

Russia had adopted the Mosin Nagant design in 1891, and with modifications this rifle/carbine system served until semi-automatic and assault rifles took over. The rifle was modified in 1930 when the barrel was shortened by several centimetres and the sights changed to a less complicated rear ramp and tunnel foresight.

A carbine model was issued in 1938, modified in 1944 by the addition of an integral folding bayonet. Designated the K44, the carbine's dimensions are: overall length – 1.01m (40 inches); barrel length – 50.8cm (20 inches); weight – 3.4kg (7lb 10oz). We have also seen 1944 carbines with 1950s dates.

The sniper version of the M1891/30 rifle was issued with either the 4x PE, or the 3.5x PU telescopic sights. The more powerful PE is the larger unit, on a two-ring side mount. The PU is much shorter overall, and sits on a single-ring side mount. In both cases, the rifle was modified by having the bolt handle extended and turned down so that it could clear the sight in operation, and a scoop of wood was removed from the right hand side to make grasping the bolt head easier. These rifles remained in service until the 1950s.

Country of origin	Russia
Calibre	7.62 x 54mm (.3 x 2.13 inches)
Overall length	1.3m (51.375 inches)
Barrel length	76.2cm (30 inches)
Weight	4.36kg (9lb 10oz)

- One-piece stock and fore-end; top handguard secured by two barrel bands; full-length clearing rod in groove
- Blade foresight and ramp rearsight, graduated to 2000 arshins (1442m – 1577 yards)
- Turning-bolt operating system
- Five-round integral box magazine, top-loaded by clip
- 3 million made in USA under contract for Russia in 1916/17

had strong hands: when they shook hands with you they had a grip like a vice.

Eventually Vasili Zaitsev was wounded in the eyes. A German sniper had taken a lot of pain to track him down. But he came back to active service and went on selecting and training snipers, his 'young hares'.

One night Soviet scouts brought in a prisoner who told them that the head of the Berlin school of snipers, a Major Konings, had been flown in to kill Zaitsev. Zaitsev later recorded that:

The arrival of the Nazi sniper set us a new task: we had to find him, study his habits and methods, and patiently await the right moment for one, and only

one, well-aimed shot. In our dug-out at nights we had furious arguments about the forthcoming duel. Every sniper put forward his speculations and guesses arising from his day's observation of the enemy's forward positions. All sorts of different proposals and 'baits' were discussed. But the art of the sniper is distinguished by the fact that whatever experience a lot of people may have, the outcome of an engagement is decided by one sniper. He meets the enemy face to face, and every time he has to create, to invent, to operate differently.

Right: This fur-hatted sniper seeking cover in front of a knocked-out T-34 is in fact a German. His attire may not be intended to deceive, but ruses of all kinds were employed by snipers on the Eastern front, including decoys, distractions and even 'live bait'.

The Russian team first had to locate the sniper from Berlin. They tried to do this by studying the style of the Nazi snipers who were firing on them. By their style of fire and camouflage the enemy snipers advertised themselves as experienced hunters or as novices, as cowards or as stubborn, determined enemies. But for some time day-by-day observations failed to reveal in which sector the man from Berlin was operating. Possibly he was altering his position frequently as he searched as carefully for Zaitsev as Zaitsev searched for him.

The breakthrough came tragically through the death of Zaitsev's friend Morozov, and the wounding of his colleague Sheykin. Morozov and Sheykin were such experienced snipers that Zaitsev felt there

could be no doubt: 'They had come up against the Nazi "super-sniper" I was looking for.'

At dawn Zaitsev and his colleague Nikolay Kulikov went to the positions these lost comrades had occupied the previous day. Inspecting the enemy's already well-studied forward positions, Zaitsev found nothing new.

The day was drawing to a close. Then above a German entrenchment unexpectedly appeared a helmet, moving slowly along a trench. Should I shoot? No! It was a trick: the helmet somehow or other moved unevenly and was presumably being held up by someone helping the sniper, while he waited for me to fire.

Somewhere before them the two men sensed that the sniper from Berlin was hiding, waiting for them to show themselves. This feeling was strongly reinforced on the third day of watching, when

Below: Snipers (particularly SS) were highly regarded by the Germans on the Eastern Front, but the Soviets used them much more. Following Vasily Zaitsev's success, the Red Army encouraged a cult of 'sniperism', feting high-scoring individuals with medals.

an army political instructor went with the two snipers to their position:

> The day dawned as usual: the light increased and minute by minute the enemy's positions could be distinguished more clearly. Battle started close by, shells hissed over us, but, glued to our telescopic sights, we kept our eyes on what was happening ahead of us.
>
> 'There he is! I'll point him out to you!' the political instructor suddenly said, excitedly. He barely, literally for one second, but carelessly, raised himself above the parapet, but that was enough for the German to hit and wound him. That sort of firing, of course, could only come from an experienced sniper.

Zaitsev examined the enemy positions. From the speed with which the German had fired, the Russian reasoned that the sniper was somewhere directly ahead. To the left was a tank, out of action, and on the right was a pill-box. He was convinced that an experienced sniper would not take up position in the tank. Nor could the German be in the pill-box, for the embrasure was closed. However, between the tank and the pill-box, on a stretch of level ground, lay a sheet of iron and a small pile of broken bricks. It had been lying there a long time and the Russians had grown accustomed to it being there. Zaitsev thought, where better for a sniper? You could make a firing slit under the sheet of metal, and then creep to and from it under the cover of darkness.

> I thought I would make sure. I put a mitten on the end of a small plank and raised it. The Nazi fell for it. I carefully let the plank down in the same position as I had raised it and examined the bullet hole. It had gone straight through from the front; that meant that the Nazi was under the sheet of metal.
>
> 'There's our viper!' came the quiet voice of Nikolay Kulikov from his hideout next to mine.

Now came the task of luring the German far enough into the open to take a shot at him. The first step was to change position during the night. The Russians were ready at dawn.

> The Germans were firing on the Volga ferries. It grew light quickly and with daybreak the battle developed with new intensity. But neither the rumble of guns nor the bursting of shells and bombs nor anything else could distract us from the job in hand.
>
> The sun rose. Kulikov took a blind shot: we had to rouse the sniper's curiosity. We had decided to spend the morning waiting, as we might have been given away by the sun on our telescopic sights. After lunch our rifles were in the shade and the sun was shining directly on to the German's position. At the edge of the sheet of metal something was glittering: an odd bit of glass or telescopic sights? Kulikov carefully, as only the most experienced can do, began to raise his helmet. The German fired. For a fraction of a second Kulikov rose and screamed. The German believed that he had finally got the Soviet sniper he had been hunting for four days, and half raised his head from beneath the sheet of metal. That was what I had been banking on. I took careful aim. The German's head fell back, and the telescopic sights of his rifle lay motionless, glistening in the sun, until night fell.

THE MORE THE MERRIER

As long as his position remains undetected, a sniper can, in theory, take out as many of the enemy as are careless enough to cross his sights. As Clifford Shore noted, not everyone who stays well-hidden and shoots carefully can strictly be accorded the title of sniper. During World War II, tenacity led many Japanese soldiers to commit a kind of *hari-kiri* by way of dedicated marksmanship combined with primitive fieldcraft. They fell victim in large numbers to a more professional approach. Shore's view of the matter was this:

Arisaka Meiji 38th Year Rifle

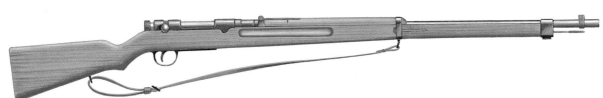

Country of origin	Japan
Calibre	65 x 50mm (2.56 x 1.97 inches)
Overall length	1.28m (50.25 inches)
Barrel length	80cm (31.375 inches)
Weight	4.3kg (9lb 8oz)

- One-piece Mauser-type shoulder stock and fore-end; separate top handguard from in front of rear sight to barrel band

- Front blade sight and rear ramp, plus 2.5x telescopic sight
- Turning-bolt operating system
- Integral five-round box magazine

The sniper variant was the Type 97. Differences are the bolt cover and the bolt handle turned down to clear the telescope, fitted to a left-side mount. A wire monopod is fitted to the barrel band; this folds forwards under the barrel when not in use to stabilise the weapon. During World War II the Type 99 replaced the 97. This was in 7.7mm (.303-inch) calibre. The sniper version was fitted with a 4x scope.

The term 'sniper' was grossly misused in connection with the Japs as it was to [refer to] the Russian sub-machine gunners and the German riflemen. The average Japanese sniper was a rifleman, and not always a good one, who had selected for himself an advantageous position from which to fire at his enemy. The true Jap sniper suitably camouflaged, specially armed and equipped with concentrated rations was responsible only for a very small amount of that which was so-often termed 'sniper fire.' It was noticed that these snipers seldom fired at parties of men larger than two or three along the jungle tracks because they feared detection by the remainder of the group, and parties of three and four men searching for these snipers by maintaining careful watch or by patrolling action had a deterrent effect.

Shore observes that the Japanese in Malaya were adept at camouflage and never shirked discomfort in achieving concealment. Their thorough training gave them 'an almost animal genius' for melting into the background. In the early part of the campaign they dressed in leaf-green uniforms – with heads and shoulders covered with green mosquito netting – a perfect match for their environment. Their helmets came with wires designed to hold camouflaging branches and grass in place. However:

There are many stories which show that the Jap, although a tenacious fighter, was very much the automaton; he was slow to react to an unexpected situation. During the Kohima affair a British sniper in the half light of early morning saw movement in a deep, narrow nullah which led to one of our forward localities. The range from his own position was only about 100 yards [90m]. With eyes riveted to the spot he saw a number of Japs crawling up the steep slopes of the nullah. This was certainly a pleasant job of work, and he immediately settled down with a stifled grunt of satisfaction, and proceeded to pick them off one by one. Immediately the first Jap had fallen to the sniper's first shot, the second man proceeded to crawl over his comrade's prostrate body. The sniper shot him, and the third man and the fourth and so on. The sniper was amazed to see that the Japs were apparently quite incapable of appreciating what was happening ... they just continued to advance, crawling over the mounting mass of corpses. The sniper finally claimed 27 killed, and when daylight came the nullah was piled high with the dead bodies.

Occasionally, however, a single shot too can have an unexpectedly fruitful effect. Former Australian soldier 'Skippy' Hampstead described one particularly

profitable incident from the 1990s, when he and a fellow mercenary were fighting for the Croats against Serb forces in the Mostar region of Bosnia. The pair carried a Steyr SSG and a Yugoslav M76:

> From one building I had a clear view of a crossroads across the river, and it was here that ... I scored my best shot of the war.
> We had been there since about 8:00am, and we'd had plenty of trade. They had absolutely no

Below: The Japanese used lone riflemen to hold up Allied advances and to ambush patrols, but in most cases they were not snipers in the true sense. This soldier stands on lookout over a bridge blown up by British and Indian troops in Burma.

Steyr-Mannlicher SSG-PI/Scharfschutzengewehr-69

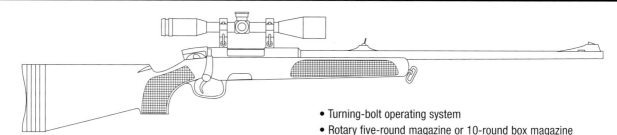

• Turning-bolt operating system
• Rotary five-round magazine or 10-round box magazine

Country of origin	Austria
Calibre	7.62 x 51mm (.3 x 2 inches), 7.823mm (.308 Winchester) and 6.172mm (.243 Winchester)
Overall length	1.14m (44.875 inches)
Barrel length	65cm (25.5 inches)
Weight	3.9kg (8lb 9oz)
Weight with telescope	4.6 kg (10lb 2oz)

• ABS Cycolac synthetic half-stock; removable spacers in butt to adjust length of pull from 32.5 to 35.5cm (12.75 inches to 14 inches)
• 6x Kahles SF69 telescopic sight (SSG-69); emergency iron sights

The SSG-69 is the issue sniper weapon in the Austrian army, and has been adopted by a number of foreign military and police forces. It was the world's first synthetic-stocked centrefire production rifle. Other features include a cold hammer-forged tapered heavy barrel, a two-stage trigger adjustable for length and weight of pull, traditional Mannlicher 'Butterknife' bolt handle, and a machined longitudinal rib on top of the receiver that accepts all types of scope mounts. The issue Kahles ZF69 telescope has an internal bullet-drop compensator graduated to 800m (875 yards); the reticle is an inverted V with broken cross hairs. The SSG-69 reportedly groups at under 2 MOA – 40cm (15.75 inches) at 800m (875 yards) – using RWS Match ammunition. The five-shot rotary magazine holds the cartridges at the shoulder for smooth feeding and to prevent damage to bullet tips during the recoil of the rifle, and has a clear backing to allow a visual count of rounds. The SSG-PI is the civilian version of the rifle.

idea where we were, so there was no return fire. About 11 o'clock a car appeared, driving very slowly towards me. 'A gift from heaven,' I thought. I aimed carefully at the driver, allowed for movement, and a metallic click of an empty chamber was the result. By the time I had reloaded, the car was gone. I was furious with myself. I had seen three men inside the car; it had been a wasted opportunity.

One cigarette and a half later the car reappeared, and turned away from me at the crossroads. Squeeze – Crack! There was a small orange flash, a boom, followed by an even bigger flash and a louder boom as the whole car blew up in a muffled explosion. I couldn't believe it. One

shot equalled three enemy soldiers, three weapons, possibly three pistols and one vehicle.

ALVIN'S AMAZING BAG

No account of sharpshooting and sniping would be complete without an appreciation of Sergeant Alvin York's renowned exploit in the Argonne Forest on the Western Front in 1918. York was not a sniper as such, but his unflinching coolness under fire, his phenomenal marksmanship and his unwavering modesty suggest that he deserves at least the honorary title.

On 8 October 1918 Corporal York was in the second platoon of an American battalion attacking German positions. At just after 0600 hours he watched in dismay as the Germans put their machines guns to work 'all over the hill in front of us and on our left and right ... I could see my pals getting picked off until it almost looked like there was none left.'

Ten days later he would record in his diary:

The Germans got us, and they got us right smart. They just stopped us dead in our tracks. It was hilly country with plenty of brush, and they had plenty of machine guns entrenched along those commanding ridges. And I'm telling you they were shooting straight. Our boys just went down like the long grass before the mowing machine at home. And, to make matters worse, something had happened to our artillery and we had no barrage.

Along with 16 others, York was sent through the brush to attempt a surprise attack from the rear against more than 30 machine guns, hidden on the ridges about 275m (300 yards) in front and on the left. The men crossed the valley, got over the enemy-held hill and reached the gully behind, where they were in the rear of a German machine-gun trench.

And when we jumped across a little stream of water that was there, they was about 15 or 20 Germans jumped up and threw up their hands and said, 'Kamerad!' So the one in charge of us boys told us not to shoot: they was going to give up anyway.

It was headquarters. There were orderlies, stretcher bearers and runners, and a major and two other officers, They were just having break-fast and there was a mess of beef-steaks, jellies, jams, and loaf bread around. They were unarmed, all except the major.

We jumped them right smart and covered them, and told them to throw up their hands and to keep them up. And they did. I guess they thought the whole American army was in their rear. And we didn't stop to tell them anything different. No shots were fired, and there was no talking between us except when we told them to 'put them up.'

By now, though, the Germans on the hill were turning their machine guns around and firing on the Americans. Soon about 30 machine guns were firing from less than 28m (30 yards). 'They couldn't miss. And they didn't!' says the diary. As the others fell, York suddenly found himself in command, but

Right: Alvin 'Sergeant' York epitomised the backwoods marksman of the Revolutionary and Civil Wars. His modesty belied his remarkable shooting, performed under stress and in the heat of battle.

pinned down in the open while the other survivors sheltered with the prisoners.

> I didn't have time to dodge behind a tree or dive into the brush, I didn't even have time to kneel or lie down ... all I could do was touch the Germans off just as fast as I could. I was sharpshooting. I don't think I missed a shot. It was no time to miss.
>
> In order to sight me or to swing their machine guns on me, the Germans had to show their heads above the trench, and every time I saw a head I just touched it off. All the time I kept yelling at them to come down. I didn't want to kill any more than I had to. But it was they or I. And I was giving them the best I had.

When a German officer and five men charged with fixed bayonets, York switched to his automatic and 'touched them off' too. 'I touched off the sixth man first, then the fifth, then the fourth, then the third and so on. I wanted them to keep coming ... I didn't want the rear ones to see me touching off the front ones. I was afraid they would drop down and pump a volley into me.'

York told the German major to tell the others to give up or he would shoot them. The major blew his whistle and nearly 100 – all but one of them – came off the hill with their hands up. The hold-out tried to kill York with a hand grenade – 'I had to touch him off.'

York discovered that he had captured the German second line and that the first line still lay between him and the American positions. 'We sure did get a long way behind the German trenches!' As he marched his prisoners towards the German front line trench, more machine guns swung around and began to fire. But, with York's automatic at his head, the German major blew his whistle and they all surrendered – 'all except one. I made the major order him

to surrender twice. But he wouldn't. And I had to touch him off. I hated to do it. But I couldn't afford to take any chances and so I had to let him have it.'

Back in his own lines York reported to Brigadier General Lindsey, who said, 'Well, York, I hear you have captured the whole damned German army.' York notes in his diary, 'I told him I only had 132.'

York, like others who have killed in the heat of

battle, seems to have been slightly bemused at the reception (which included a ticker-tape parade in New York City) that followed his exploit. For the sniper, bringing death to an enemy carries no less an intensity of awareness, but it is one of a different order. Lt Col Thomas D. Ferran summed it up in words that epitomise the uniqueness, the courage and the solitude of the sniper's vocation:

Sniping is a very personal experience. You look through your scope and you see what the person looks like. You realise they are human. You've got complete control over their life, you've become God like, in that once you pull that trigger and take them out – you just owned their life. As a sniper you carry that 'last sight picture' with you for the rest of your life.

INDEX

PICTURE CREDITS

Aerospace Publishing Ltd: 44-45, 76, 82, 100-101. **Novosti (London):** 49. **Robert Hunt Library:** 28, 166-167, 178. **Salamander Picture Library:** 12, 18. **Frank Spooner Pictures Ltd:** 55, 56, 72-73, 75, 78, 96, 98-99, 102-103, 104-105, 106, 114-115, 126-127, 128, 136, 140, 142, 154. **TRH Pictures:** 6-7, 8, 10, 13, 17, 19 (US National Archives), 20 (US National Archives), 21 (US National Archives), 23, 27, 31 (IWM), 32, 34-35, 36-37, 38 (US Dept of Defense), 40 (US Marine Core), 41 (US Dept of Defense), 47 (US National Archives), 50-51 (US National Archives), 52 (IWM), 59 (US Marine Core), 60-61 (US Marine Core), 63, 64 (US National Archives), 65, 66-67 (IWM), 68 (US National Archives), 69, 70 (IWM), 81 (US Dept of Defense), 85, 87, 91 (US Navy), 92 (US Army), 95 (US Marine Core), 110, 113 (US Marine Core), 116, 117 (US Marine Core), 118, 119, 122 (Royal Marines), 129, 148-149, 156-157, 158 (both), 159 (US National Archives), 161, 163, 165, 168-169 (US Marine Core), 170-171 (US Dept of Defense), 173, 174 (US Marine Core), 176 (IWM), 177 (US National Archives), 181, 182, 185, 187. **P. Valpolini:** 42, 86, 109, 112, 121, 123, 132-133, 134, 141, 144-145, 150, 151, 152. **VS-Books/Carl Schulze:** 88-89, 107, 120, 188-189.

Artworks:

De-Agostini UK Ltd: 124, 146, 147.
John Batchelor: 11, 26, 30, 33, 62, 180, 184.
Bob Garwood: 57, 90, 108, 111, 131, 137, 139, 143, 153(both), 155, 164, 186.
Orbis Publishing: 15, 24, 39, 53, 71, 80, 94 (both), 160.
Salamander: 48.

Picture research: TRH Pictures; Jim Winchester; Lisa Wren